FOUNDATIONS

OF A *Free* & *Virtuous* SOCIETY

DYLAN PAHMAN

FOUNDATIONS

OF A *Free* & *Virtuous* SOCIETY

ACTONINSTITUTE

All Scripture quotations, unless otherwise noted, are taken from the New King James Version® (NKJV). Copyright © 1982 by Thomas Nelson. Used by permission. All rights reserved.

ISBN 978-1-942503-54-5

Cover by Scaturro Design
Interior composition by Judy Schafer

ACTONINSTITUTE

98 E. Fulton
Grand Rapids, Michigan 49503
Phone: 616.454.3080
www.acton.org

Printed in the United States of America

Contents

Foreword

How we understand God, the human person, and human society, which includes philosophy, politics, economics, and civil society, will determine much of how we think about everything. This is the central thesis of this short book by Dylan Pahman. A corollary of that thesis is that a great deal of political, economic, and philosophical error and social disorder will result if we proceed on the basis of erroneous concepts of God and man. If, for instance, we view people as uncreative, essentially unfree, unresponsive to incentives, or needing constant top-down direction, it is highly likely that we will gravitate toward a socialist, even statist, view of political, legal, and economic policy.

People's capacity to understand this basic truth about human beings and human society, one that might be described as anthropological, has been compromised by many developments in recent decades. One is that most people who attend university do not engage in the systematic type of study that methodically unfolds the relationships among such things. The same attendance at university is also likely to be highly specialized in nature. A student may receive, for instance, a thorough, even sophisticated, immersion in theology and philosophy, yet learn virtually nothing about economics—or vice versa. As a result, that student may fall into the trap of thinking about everything theologically (which is not wrong in itself) but with complete unawareness that economics can provide us with insights into the human condition that theology, by itself, cannot—and vice versa.

One of the Acton Institute's concerns, from its beginning, has been to provide people of all confessions across the world with this type of integrated approach to understanding the human condition in light of the fullness of truth that we find in Divine Revelation and reason. Starting with an outline of basic truths about the nature of human beings, it has sought to unfold the implications of seeing man as a creative, rational, free, individual, social, and sinful being for economic life, associational activity, the role and character of the state, and international affairs, especially international economic relations.

The conclusions that people will reach about many of these areas will be prudential, inasmuch as there is considerable room for disagreement among Jews, Christians, and people of other faiths concerning these subjects. You cannot go, for example, straight from the truths of Christian anthropology to a determination that the ideal maximum income tax rate is 40 percent—or 80 percent or 2 percent. But you will start to see that there are tax rates that undermine initiative and disincentivize people from being creative in economic life. Similarly, Christian anthropology will not tell you what is the optimal political system or form of government. It will, however, let us know that those governmental forms that severely block human beings' opportunity to make free choices set the state against a basic feature of human anthropology. In short, Christian anthropology indicates that, while there are legitimate arguments about what the limits of state power ought to be, the preference ought to be for *limited* rather than totalitarian government.

These are not new insights. People have been speaking and writing about Christian anthropology and its implications for social, economic, and political order for centuries. But while there are many books and articles that have been written in this area, very few have been written for general audiences and even fewer have been composed with an eye to simplicity in explanation.

Unusual, too, is the book's ecumenical approach. Pahman draws upon evangelical, Orthodox, mainline Protestant, and Catholic documents, as well as sources that are common to all of these confessions. Complemented by a style that makes complex theological, political, and economic ideas easily comprehensible, Pahman's careful explanation of the relationship between Christian anthropology and concerns for freedom, justice, development, and human flourishing will be accessible to people of varying religious and educational backgrounds.

Pahman thus demonstrates that economics in general and free market economics in particular are not especially difficult to understand. Christians and other people of faith are often inclined to see economics as very complicated or, in some instances, as reflecting and generating a view of human beings that verges on the antihuman. Pahman shows, however, that economics is the study and application of certain insights into the human condition and the functioning of particular human institutions. Prominent among these are the role of incentives, the idea of comparative advantage, the workings of trade-offs, and how free prices convey information about the supply and demand of literally billions of products and services at any one point in time. The importance of institutions that many Christians tend to take for granted—most notably, private property and the rule of law—is also underscored by Pahman who shows just how much functioning economies depend on their long-term strength. This is especially true when it comes to an issue that all Christians must take seriously, which is poverty and poverty-alleviation.

One of Christianity's most important messages is that it is folly to try and create earthly utopias, something well-summed up in the slogan *Don't Immanentize the Eschaton!* Pahman shows that this error is made repeatedly by many Christians, some of whom have acted in such a way on the basis of good intentions. At the same time, this short text shows how Christians can effect meaningful and lasting change *if* they take the truths revealed by their own faith in the human condition seriously and *if* they also pay attention to the insights that everyone, believer and nonbeliever, can find in the economic way of thinking. Neither economics as a social science nor free markets as the embodiment of particular economic practices and certain political, legal, and social institutions, will save our souls. But, informed and directed by an understanding of Christian anthropology, which

Christians believe is the full truth about man, human life can be made more humane—including in the economy. If that is the only message that readers take away from this book, it will have helped to realize a great end.

Samuel Gregg
Director of Research
Acton Institute

Introduction

Today we need a maximum of specialized economic understanding, but also a maximum of ethos so that specialized economic understanding may enter the service of the right goals.

—Joseph Cardinal Ratzinger[1]

Setting the Stage

It is not uncommon for people today, Christians especially perhaps, to champion the values of faith and freedom, no matter what their tradition, political orientation, or moral vision may be. But the policies and practices that follow from and contribute to those values are not self-evident. Well-intentioned people including those with genuine faith in Jesus Christ can be found on all sides of every political, cultural, economic, and sometimes even moral issue.

This book is hardly meant to conclusively settle any such debates. Rather, the goal is to elucidate one common starting point that aims to promote a free and virtuous society and only one take on that perspective in particular: my own. Thus, this book is meant to be an introductory work of Christian social thought. It should work as a bridge to help people get from point A (Judeo-Christian values) to point B (a free society) in a way that doesn't descend into impracticality or fail to regard the rich heritage of the past. As Christ himself put it, "every scribe instructed concerning the kingdom of heaven is like a house-holder who brings out of his treasure things new and old" (Matt. 13:52). That is my aspiration, at least.

In particular, the focus is to bridge the gap between faith and economics, though the broader concept of "political economy" might be a more accurate term. This is not because other areas of concern are less important. Some are more important, and many will be touched on here. Nevertheless, as economic issues tend to be divisive enough on their own, outlining a careful framework for approaching such issues is a big and an important enough task for one little book.

Therefore, on the one hand ...

Economics Matters

When people of goodwill seek to help the poor without proper knowledge of economics, they can end up doing more harm than good, thus perpetuating the problem they sought to solve.

For example, take fair trade coffee. Henderson State University economist Victor Claar has written a brief treatment, *Fair Trade? Its Prospects as a Poverty Solution*. A post on the website of the FairChain Foundation describes Dr. Claar as follows:

> Victor Claar is the kind of guy that gets up at the crack of dawn each day, eats a bloody steak for breakfast and washes it down with eight raw eggs. After that he goes for a barefoot morning run over jagged stones and hot coals, wrestles a saber tooth tiger and then goes to meet Mike Tyson for brunch where he fearlessly gives him boxing pointers. At least, that's the equivalent of what he's doing in the world of economics. To put it simply, you can think of him as Chuck Norris in a suit.
>
> So when Victor Claar raises an eyebrow over the eco-nomic and moral problems underlying the fair trade coffee movement that he believes are holding impoverished cof-fee farmers in a poverty cycle—his words are to be noted.[2]

Okay, so that may be a *little* hyperbolic. But the point is that Victor Claar knows what he's talking about.

Most of us have seen the Fair Trade label on coffee and other goods in the supermarket. But how does it really work? In his book, where he focuses on coffee in particular, Claar describes the aims of the movement as follows:

> The idea behind fair trade is a simple, compassionate one. Rich northern consumers pay a little extra for coffee that has been certified to satisfy fair trade standards.... Through their purchases of fair trade coffee, consumers presumably engage in "ethical consumption," using the coffee market itself as a means of voting for better treatment of southern coffee growers. The primary guarantee of the fair trade label is that the coffee bearing its mark has been produced by individual or family growers—working within a cooperative—who receive a minimum-price guarantee for their crop.[3]

Sounds good, doesn't it? Many churches, denominations, and other religious groups have openly endorsed it and committed themselves to buying only fair trade coffee. Not only does it pursue the good intention of helping poor coffee farmers, it even seeks to help them through the market! First World people pay a little extra to buy coffee that is certified fair, believing that they are adding to their lattes two tablespoons of sweet, sweet justice because Third World farmers get a better price. Win-win. Right?

Claar begins his analysis by giving some background on the coffee business. He describes how both supply and demand for coffee tends to be inelastic in the short run. What that means is whether prices go up or down people still drink about the same amount of coffee a day. Similarly, when demand does increase or decrease, coffee growers are unable to respond by increasing or decreasing supply fast enough—coffee plants take two to five years to grow and then produce a crop perennially for about ten years. Growers cannot increase the number of bean producing plants in a quick enough time to benefit from short jumps in demand. Furthermore, over the *long-term* (the last few decades) supply *has* increased, which has driven prices down for growers.

Thus, Claar summarizes their plight:

> Indeed, if someone is currently growing coffee, we can
> safely presume that is his best available option. If it were
> not, he would be doing something else instead. Yet, grow-
> ing coffee pays poorly. Moreover, due to the synergy of
> demand and supply inelasticities, a coffee grower faces
> tremendous risk and uncertainty at the start of a growing
> season because coffee prices can fluctuate dramatically
> over quite short periods of time. A grower simply cannot
> forecast with much certainty the price at which he will be
> able to sell his crop.

So here is where the fair trade movement markets itself as the
solution, "guaranteeing both higher prices and greater price
stability."[4] But does that work? Does it really help these coffee
farmers?

Unfortunately, no. Among other reasons, Claar explains that

> the fair trade movement, for all its good intentions, can-
> not deliver on what it promises. Simply put, coffee grow-
> ers are poor because there is too much coffee. Fair trade
> simply does not address that fundamental reality. In fact,
> by guaranteeing a price to growers that is higher than the
> world price of coffee, fair trade makes the supply of cof-
> fee even larger than it would otherwise be.... [W]henever
> coffee prices increase, there will be another coffee grower,
> and another, and another.[5]

As of 2004, the price tag for cooperatives to get fair trade certifi-
cation came in at a hefty $3,200. Single growers, large or small,
who are not a part of a cooperative cannot qualify based on fair
trade standards. Thus, only about one percent of coffee growers
are part of fair trade cooperatives. Only about 20 percent of the
coffee these cooperatives grow is sold through fair trade chan-
nels. And then, only a tiny amount of the upcharge on the average five-dollar fair trade Frappuccino actually makes it down
the chain to the growers themselves.

As a result, writes Claar, "fair trade agreements act like golden
handcuffs that bind the wrists of fair trade cooperatives and

their member growers." How? "Fair trade discourages member growers from trying something new that they would certainly otherwise try if they did not have the security of the fair trade price."[6] That is, those same farmers could be growing and selling more profitable crops, but they are drawn to fair trade by the promise of a stable price that is (albeit minimally) higher than other coffee growers. Thinking they are getting a better deal, they remain in poverty by growing and selling a crop that will never sell at prices that could make a significant difference in their incomes.

Alas, this is just one of countless examples of people with good, truly moral, intentions that cause more harm than good due to a lack of basic economic knowledge. So economics is important.

But on the other hand …

Economics Is Not Enough

In the 1930s, in a series of articles on the topic of ethics and economic reform, the economist Frank Knight, one of the founders of the Chicago school of economics, insisted that "without an adequate ethics and sociology in the broad sense, economics has little to say about policy."[7] That is, without some basic understanding of what constitutes the best life for a person to live (ethics) and the makeup of human society and human social behavior (sociology), how can economists make recommendations for what policies human economies *ought* to be guided by?

Now, Knight wasn't optimistic about the potential of Christian theology for filling that need. But it is also safe to say that the form of Christian ethics he critiqued was not and is not the only one. From a Christian point of view, we cannot rightly understand the purpose of our lives and the nature of human society without first understanding human nature as God created it and as it currently is. As Jordan Ballor, a research fellow and colleague at the Acton Institute, put it, "When severed from questions of transcendence posed by theology, economics loses its way and, like other forms of worldly wisdom, sets itself up as the leading principle or standard-bearer for ultimate truth and reality." This temptation is called *economism*, which Ballor defines as the viewpoint "in which the only acceptable explanatory phenomena are economic in nature; everything else is epiphenomenal and ultimately dispensable."[8]

Observing this myopic tendency in his own time, the Russian Orthodox economist-turned-theologian Sergei Bulgakov asserted, "In practice, economists are Marxists, even if they hate Marxism."[9] That is, while Karl Marx did not believe that life was only economic, he did believe that material causes were ultimate. Everything in life, he believed, could be traced to one's economic or social reality. He wrote that "the social history of men is never anything but the history of their individual development, whether they are conscious of it or not. Their material relations are the basis of all their relations."[10]

On the one hand, we have already seen that Marx was right to emphasize that all of life has an economic aspect, and economists today, even those who hate Marxism, are right to emphasize the same point. Without acknowledging the economic dimension to our lives and giving it the attention it deserves, we end up running into situations, like fair trade coffee, where we think we're doing something good but are actually making things worse.

On the other hand, though, it is quite naïve to imagine that all of life—including love, beauty, truth, faith, happiness, hatred, ugliness, falsehood, denial, tragedy, and so on—is ultimately reducible to economic concerns. As Knight would put it, "Life is economic; economics is not all of life."[11] Economics is an amazing and indispensable tool for analyzing one aspect of life. But it cannot tell us about what goals that tool should be used for. One may be a master carpenter (so, not me) who can operate hammers, saws, and drills with precision and ease, but without some *plan* for what is to be built (say, one provided by an architect), those tools would rarely be put to use. Similarly, when it comes to public policy, economics needs something from outside itself to provide the ends for which it ought to be used, the vision of what sort of society it ought to serve. As the economist Friedrich Hayek put it, "[N]obody can be a great economist who is only an economist—and I am even tempted to add that the economist who is only an economist is likely to become a nuisance if not a positive danger."[12]

Thus, it is at our peril that we so commonly separate faith and morality from economics, and vice versa. Ballor summarizes the predicament well:

> [O]ne might think of the old saw that an economist is the cynic of Oscar Wilde's description: someone who "knows the price of everything, and the value of nothing." Likewise, the theologian may be seen as the sentimentalist, according to Wilde, one "who sees an absurd value in everything, and doesn't know the market price of any single thing."[13]

The purpose of this book is to help people, in whatever vocation God has called them, to not only see the necessary connection between these facets of life but also to gain some basic competency in how to better integrate faith, morality, and social science. The modest hope is that readers might be able to move beyond cynicism and sentimentality toward a more holistic approach to the social, and specifically economic, problems of our time.

What Next?

Consistent with this book's theological orientation, we can highlight the following three relationships that correspond to the first three chapters:

1. Humanity before God
2. Human beings with their neighbors
3. Humanity and the world

Each topic informs the next. Thus, while economics is concerned with proper cultivation of the resources of the earth, cultivation is done *within* human communities and *under* God. Similarly, human communities are not ends in themselves but are subject to the constraints of human nature—created by God in his image and for his glory though damaged by sin and in need of salvation. The second part of the book further integrates these three by exploring what happens when we ignore basic insights of economic science.

In examining these three headings, I endeavor to take a "mere Christian" approach, to use the phrase of C. S. Lewis.[14] This book is thus self-consciously ecumenical. Nevertheless, I am an Orthodox Christian by tradition, and at times, against my intentions, it is possible for that perspective to overshadow Protestant and Roman Catholic viewpoints.

Furthermore, in an appendix to this book I have included (with brief explanations) the Acton Institute's ten core principles. This book was conceived as a way to introduce inquirers to Acton's approach to the integration of faith and free markets represented by those principles, and all of them in substance will be touched on herein.

To sum up the forgoing as I proceed to the body of my text, I will borrow Victor Claar's own conclusion to *Fair Trade?*

> Jesus does not command that we love him with some arbitrary combination of any or all of our hearts, *or* our souls, *or* our strength, *or* our minds. He commands that we serve him with all that we have, together with our minds.
>
> By bringing the clear economic thinking of our minds to bear on the matters that tug hardest at our hearts and souls, we will serve him—and his children everywhere—as he commands.[15]

May this little book be a tool to that end.

Notes

1. Joseph Cardinal Ratzinger, "Church and Economy: Responsibility for the Future of the World Economy," trans. Stephen Wentworth Arndt, *Communio* 13, no. 3 (Fall 1986): 204.

2. "Is Fair Trade Curing Poverty?" FairChain Foundation, April 30, 2015, http://fairchain.org/?p=509.

3. Victor V. Claar, *Fair Trade? Its Prospects as a Poverty Solution* (Grand Rapids: PovertyCure, 2012), 1–2.

4. Claar, *Fair Trade?*, 19.

5. Claar, *Fair Trade?*, 50.

6. Claar, *Fair Trade?*, 52.

7. Frank H. Knight, "Ethics and Economic Reform: III. Christianity," *Economica*, New Series 6, no. 24 (November 1939): 422.

8. Jordan J. Ballor, "Theology and Economics: A Match Made in Heaven?" *Journal of Interdisciplinary Studies* 26, no. 1/2 (2014): 123.

9. Sergei Bulgakov, *Philosophy of Economy: The World as Household*, trans. Catherine Evtuhov (1912; repr., New Haven and London: Yale University Press, 2000), 41.

10. Karl Marx, "Society and Economy in History," in *The Marx-Engels Reader*, 2nd ed., edited by Robert C. Tucker (New York; London: Norton & Company, 1978), 137.

11. Ross B. Emmett, "Economics Is Not All of Life," *Econ Journal Watch* 11, no. 2 (May 2014): 146. Emmett is here summarizing Knight.

12. F. A. Hayek, "The Dilemma of Specialization," in Hayek, *Studies in Philosophy, Politics and Economics* (New York: Touchstone, 1969), 123.

13. Ballor, "Theology and Economics," 123.

14. See C. S. Lewis, *Mere Christianity* (New York: Harper & Row, 1952).

15. Claar, *Fair Trade?*, 61–62.

Part 1

CHRISTIAN ANTHROPOLOGY

1

What Does It Mean to Be Human?

How then is man, this mortal, passible, short-lived being, the image of that nature which is immortal, pure, and everlasting?

—St. Gregory of Nyssa[1]

Introduction

In one of Bill Waterson's *Calvin and Hobbes* comic strips, six-year-old Calvin stands flexing his arms in front of a mirror wearing only his underwear. "Made in God's own image, yes sir!" he boasts. Meanwhile his stuffed tiger Hobbes, whom Calvin always imagines is a real, full grown tiger, speculates, "God must have a goofy sense of humor." There is something a bit silly about the idea that we reflect God's image, isn't there?

I wonder if Waterson had Mark Twain in mind when he drew that strip. Twain once wrote,

> There are many pretty and winning things about the human race. It is perhaps the poorest of all the inventions of all the gods but it has never suspected it once. There is nothing prettier than its naive and complacent appreciation of itself. It comes out frankly and proclaims without bashfulness or any sign of a blush that it is the

> noblest work of God. It has had a billion opportunities to
> know better, but all signs fail with this ass. I could say
> harsh things about it but I cannot bring myself to do it—it
> is like hitting a child.[2]

Perhaps we're just full of ourselves. Are we all, like Calvin, just little children standing in front of a mirror and imagining our own glory? Twain was especially troubled by all of the terrible things human beings have done, especially Christians. Rightly so. Yet, I do think there is something more to God's goofy little joke we call the human race.

Whole books have been written in an attempt to answer the question, "What does it mean to be human?" One little chapter can hardly offer a comprehensive answer, though as a small consolation, I remind myself that we are, to quote the psalmist, "fearfully and wonderfully made" (Ps. 139:14). Can anyone really be comprehensive? God knows the depths of our being, but "such knowledge is too wonderful for me" (Ps. 139:6).

Instead of attempting the impossible, then, I'm going to focus on some basics of Judeo-Christian anthropology. In particular, in this chapter, I want to focus on the significance of God's statement, "Let Us make man in Our image, according to Our likeness" (Gen. 1:26). We will continue to discuss what it means to be human in chapters 2 and 3. But for now, this will be enough.

So what has Genesis told us about God up to this point that might inform our understanding of his image? Surely an ancient reader, like anyone today, would have had their own preconceptions of God, some sense of the supernatural and some idea of what it was. Speculating about what that may have been is a valuable exercise, but beyond the scope of this book. Rather, what does the text *itself* tell us about God? And, since we are God's creatures, what does it tell us about his creation? Putting the two together ought to get us pretty close to a basic answer to this chapter's question.

What does the text tell us about God?

First, it seems pretty clear and uncontroversial to say that God makes stuff: "In the beginning God created the heavens and the earth" (Gen. 1:1). And up to our verse 26, he's still making things. So God is creative. He's free, imaginative, and powerful.

Second, God is rational. He knows what makes sense and what does not, and he does the former but not the latter. He's logical. Now some might balk at this as imposing a later concept of God upon the biblical text, but there's plenty of support for it in Genesis 1. There are at least three pieces of evidence there:

(1) God speaks: "Then God said, 'Let there be light'; and there was light" (Gen. 1:3). Language follows a logical structure. It has syntax and conjugation. It is used to categorize things, to make sense of the world. As the Russian Orthodox philosopher Vladimir Solovyov put it, "The word is the instrument of reason for expressing that which is."[3] And how true for God! For him, it apparently is the instrument for making things *be* in the first place. Indeed, the Gospel According to John even says that "the Word [*logos*] was God" (John 1:1). So when Genesis says God speaks, which is an action in accord with logic, it reveals how the Word or *Logos* is God.

(2) Not only does he make things by speaking, God judges what he made: "And God saw the light, that it was good" (Gen. 1:4). God assesses the light as good and beautiful. He appreciates it. Just as he did by giving it a name and speaking it into being, he puts it in another category: "good." But he could not judge it to be good if he did not have the ability to distinguish between what makes sense according to the category "good" and what does not. Thus, this judgment is a rational exercise as well and evidence that God is rational.

(3) Not only does he make and judge things, God orders them: "God divided the light from the darkness" (Gen. 1:4). Ordering, dividing, grouping—this again is an act of categorization and thus of reason. God distinguishes the light from the darkness, the water above from the water below, the land from the seas. Everything has its place, and God knows it and puts it all right where it belongs.

Third, we need to answer another question: What do we know at this point about God's creation? The text tells us at least four things:

(1) Apart from God's ordering it, creation is chaos. Thus, after God creates the earth, it is described as being something of a mess on its own: "The earth was without form, and void; and darkness was on the face of the deep" (Gen. 1:2). According to many

biblical scholars, the Hebrew phrase for "without form and void" (*tohu wa bohu*) is an idiom that means "chaotic." So one way of looking at the rest of the story is how God creates order instead of chaos. He doesn't just make stuff; he makes a cosmos, which means "order." We might even think of God as a cosmetologist (from the same Greek root as *cosmos*), because he adorns what he made with beauty.

(2) Creation is subordinate to God. It does what he says. He says for something to exist, and like a soldier taking a command, it does as it is told. He tells the land to produce plants and animals, and that's exactly what happens, which brings me to my third point.

(3) God makes each thing "according to its kind" (Gen. 1:11, 12, 21, 24, 25). Everything exists according to his plan. Things have a design, a nature, a "kind." Dogs and cats are animals— that's one kind they share in common. Yet, dogs are not cats. A cat is a cat, and a dog is a dog. The nature "dog" is not shared by cats. Natures are all the essentials of what a thing is. Change one essential property, and you've got something else with a different nature. If God had made us with the legs and horns of goats, for example, we'd be fauns, not humans (though we'd still be mammals). And so on.

(4) Creation is subject to time: "And there was evening and there was morning, one day" (Gen. 1:5 RSV). More accurately, perhaps, creation is subject to change, and time is a measure of the movements of our ever-changing universe. Everything God makes moves and grows and expands and contracts, at least on a molecular level. At one time it's one way, and then at the next it's different. This also is essential to what it means to be part of God's creation and not the Creator himself.

So humanity is somehow like both of these, God and creation. We are made in the image of God, who is free and creative and reasonable, yet we are also *made*. We are a part of this creation that is subordinate to God, is chaotic without him, has natures, and is subject to time and change. But all in all, that doesn't sound too bad, does it? If only the story ended there, right? Alas, there's more. To cut to the chase (see Genesis 3), we are also subject to corruption, sin, and death. We are meant to grow in our likeness to God according to the nature he gave us, but too often we do the opposite and obscure the beauty of his image within us.

So, for the purposes of this book, I offer the following answer to this chapter's question: To be human means that we are *made in the image of God as free, rational animals, but we are corrupted by sin and death*. Let's break this definition down further.

Free

I start with freedom because there is a sense in which we cannot be called rational if we are not also free. As the eighth-century church father St. John of Damascus put it in his compendium of Christian teaching, "either man is an irrational being, or, if he is rational, he is master of his acts and endowed with free-will."[4] That is, it doesn't make sense for someone to have the power to judge what choices are better or worse than others without also having the power to choose one thing and not another. For practical purposes, our reason would be wasted, and then we wouldn't really be rational at all, just robotic. Historically, this is something consistently affirmed by Jewish and Christian theologians, in contrast to many who, even today, claim that free will is no more than an illusion.

What does it mean to be free? There are probably about a dozen right answers to that question. I'll start, however, with the most basic: *able to make choices*.

Those of us who were American children in the 1980s and 1990s likely remember the wildly popular Choose Your Own Adventure book series, featuring such titles as *The Forbidden Castle*, *House of Danger*, and *Inside UFO 54-40*. Daniel Silliman, a postdoctoral teaching fellow in the Department of History at the University of Notre Dame, whose dissertation work was on contemporary evangelical fiction, has pointed out that "there was a very serious religious idea behind those popular children's books."[5] He explains.

> They engaged readers with [series co-creator R. A.] Montgomery's core belief, illustrating again and again a central value of human agency and responsibility.

"It's finally saying to you, *you're* involved," Montgomery said in one of the few interviews he did on the subject. "What are you doing and why are you making these choices?"

In 1958–1959, Montgomery was a student at Yale Divinity School. "In his short time there," writes Silliman,

> he became acquainted with the school's chaplain, William Sloane Coffin, who had a huge impact on Montgomery. In the last years of his life, writing on his personal blog, Montgomery would frequently quote Coffin, calling him "my old friend Bill."
>
> Coffin, a liberal Protestant in the Social Gospel tradition, believed that being a minister of the gospel required him to be an activist and an advocate of social justice.

This inspired Montgomery to focus on teaching people about the importance of individual choices, sometimes to the chagrin of those who would rather focus on unjust social structures. According to Silliman, "the books opened with a warning that captured the core of Montgomery's spiritual-but-not-religious humanism: 'BEWARE and WARNING! You and YOU ALONE are in charge of what happens in this story!'"

Now, obviously our concern above with Genesis places us outside of the "spiritual-but-not-religious" approach, but Montgomery's basic idea was right. All day, every day, we are faced with choices and, by all appearances at least, we have it in our own power to make those choices.

Montgomery gets at something a bit deeper too. *Freedom entails responsibility*. We don't just get to make our own choices, we have to live with the consequences of those choices, and we are rightly held accountable for them. As St. John of Damascus put it, "Voluntariness, then, is assuredly followed by praise or blame."[6] Thus, God exhorts Israel, "I have set before you life and death, blessing and cursing; therefore choose life, that both you and your descendants may live" (Deut. 30:19).

One way in which we grow in the likeness of God is by making good choices; becoming good like God, the source of all life and blessing. The British lord and Roman Catholic John Acton once remarked that "the Catholic notion" of liberty is "not the power of doing what we like, but the right of being able to do what we ought."[7] Similarly, Benjamin Franklin said that "only a virtuous people are capable of freedom."[8] Easier said than done, of course, but I'll get to that later.

To recap, freedom means to be able to make choices, and that means being responsible for what we choose to do. Yet it is not as if we can therefore do *anything*. Our freedom is limited in a variety of ways, the first of which is our own nature. As humans we are naturally free to make our own choices, but we can only do things that humans are naturally capable of doing. Thus, for example, apart from the assistance of technology or a miracle, I am incapable of flying. I'm a man and not an angel. I have two arms and two legs but, alas, zero wings. In the same way, I can't breathe underwater either. I have two lungs, but zero gills. I am not a merman.

Our choices are also limited by our circumstances. I *could* buy my own private jet, if I could afford it. But I can't. My buying choices are bound by my financial circumstances. I *could* paint a replica of Raphael's Sistine Madonna if I were a skilled enough painter. But I'm not. My artistic choices are bound by my artistic ability. Saint John of Damascus gives an excellent illustration of his own:

> Notice that there are certain things that occupy a place intermediate between what is voluntary and what is involuntary. Although they are unpleasant and painful we welcome them as the escape from a still greater trouble; for instance, to escape shipwreck we cast the cargo overboard."[9]

Sometimes the best we can do in a given circumstance is to choose between the better of two bad options.

Finally, for now, our choices are also limited by our choices themselves. Economists call this opportunity cost. If my wife Kelly and I go on a date this week, we will have less money in our monthly budget for other fun stuff. So the choice to go on a date this week eliminates the possibility of using the same resources for other things. Similarly, if I choose to hang out with friends one night, I cannot also go on a date with Kelly that same night. As part of God's creation, we are temporal beings. We busy Americans know all about this. We're used to thoughts like this: "Okay, I can fit in coffee with Fred next Tuesday right *after* dropping off Sally at daycare and *before* my afternoon dentist appointment with Dr. Pain." Or how many of us on Facebook reply "maybe" or "interested" to nearly every RSVP? We want to do everything, but we can't. Choosing some things means not choosing others.

The ancient Stoic philosopher Epictetus even emphasized that often our own unhappiness comes from unreasonable expectations about what we can or cannot do: "Do you now desire that which is possible and that which is possible to you? Why then are you hindered? why are you unhappy?"[10] Even if we might not agree with every point of his ethics, it is fair to say that being honest about the limitations of our freedom can save us from a lot of self-inflicted grief, not to mention keeping us grounded in the real world.

Epictetus's idea reminds me of when my son Brendan, at three and a half, would occasionally have a breakdown because we wouldn't let him drive our car. Even if we were foolish enough to let him, it wouldn't be possible. His legs were too short, and he couldn't see over the steering wheel. But before laughing about those times, perhaps I ought to ask myself how often I'm no better. Do I ever grieve because I don't have something I can't afford in the first place? Or am I frustrated because I don't have time to do all the things I want to? Well, then I'm being childish too. Brendan, at least, has the excuse of being an actual child.

Rational

What does it mean to be rational? I've already covered a little of this above: It means to be able to categorize, to order, to reflect, and to judge. But we can be more specific than that. Because I find him so clear and straightforward, I'll start again with St. John of Damascus:

> [R]eason consists of a speculative and a practical part. The speculative part is the contemplation of the nature of things, and the practical consists in deliberation and

defines the true reason for what is to be done. The speculative side is called mind or wisdom, and the practical side is called reason or prudence.[11]

Now we're getting somewhere. Reason is that mental faculty that allows us to identify what things are (wisdom) and consider and determine what must be done (prudence). Let's start with wisdom.

In the late nineteenth and early twentieth centuries, there lived a man in the Netherlands who only comes along once or twice in a generation. His name was Abraham Kuyper. He was a journalist, editing two newspapers and serving as chairman of the Dutch Association of Journalists from 1898 to 1901. He was a pastor and theologian, founding his own Calvinist denomination and writing extensive tomes on all sorts of theological topics. He was a politician, founding and heading his own political party and even serving as prime minister from 1901 to 1905. He was an educator, founding the Free University of Amsterdam. To say he was ambitious is an understatement. In fact, he may have occasionally overestimated his capabilities, suffering a few nervous breakdowns in his time. He also never slept and ate only prepackaged space food while in transit from one responsibility to another. Okay, so that last part is just my own (reasonable) speculation. But the point is that Kuyper was amazing and was himself amazingly knowledgeable. No doubt few readers could agree with everything he ever wrote, but his writing is full of remarkable insights. He is an excellent example of wisdom.

Reflecting on the biblical story of creation, Kuyper argued that because everything exists by God's will, thought, and word, it "forces upon us the recognition of something that is general, hidden and yet expressed in that which is general. Yea, it forces us to the confession that there must be stability and regularity ruling over everything."[12] God, who is rational, created a rational order to the world and made us in his image as rational beings. Thus, he made us able to discern that order through our speculative reason or wisdom.

To Kuyper, this is the theological foundation of science. Or, as the psalmist put it, "The heavens declare the glory of God; and the firmament shows His handiwork" (Ps. 19:1). Not only can we discover that order, but we can also imitate it in our own creations. So we could say that it's the theological grounding of engineering too. Thus, though I cannot naturally fly like a bird, I can with an airplane. Though I cannot naturally breathe underwater like a fish, I can with scuba gear. In such creations, the fruits of scientific inquiry and ingenuity, we imitate God's own creation of the world through the free use of our own rational natures.

Similarly, despite unfounded stereotypes to the contrary, artists also demonstrate rationality working together with freedom to create beauty. As the sociologist Peter Berger put it, with a different subject in mind, "The botanist looking at a daffodil has no reason to dispute the right of the poet to look at the same object in a very different manner. There are many ways of playing."[13] In fact, when Genesis says, "Then God saw everything that He had made, and indeed it was very good" (Gen. 1:31), the word *good* could also be translated "beautiful." Thus, art shares the same theological grounding as science. Inspired by the beauty of God's orderly creation, and mixed with their own creativity and reason, artists create new worlds of beauty in imitation of God, continuing his divine cosmetology of the universe. Of course many artists also create out of artistic feeling and intuition, yet, as we shall see below, that does not necessarily make such creations irrational. First, however, we need to address prudence.

Prudence is sometimes misrepresented. For example, I've heard it said that such-and-such social issue is not a moral matter but a matter of prudence. What the person who said that more likely meant was that the issue was not one of *principle*. But prudence is a virtue, and thus prudential matters are most certainly moral. Prudence is what tells us, to use St. John of Damascus's example above, that for the love of the people aboard a sinking ship, we should "cast the cargo overboard." Not only would people be mistaken if they insisted on trying to save the cargo, they'd be immoral and irrational. They'd be immoral because they'd value things more than people (which incidentally is not a bad definition of greed). They'd be irrational because keeping the cargo but not the people probably isn't an option anyway. Keeping the cargo means the ship, *with the cargo* and everything else aboard it, would sink. Due to their circumstances, such people would not be free to save the cargo no matter what they did.

Prudence, then, is not about definitions or abstract concepts like speculative reason. It should be informed by the right principles and definitions, but it is not reducible to them. Prudence is the ability to make the best choice in less-than-ideal circumstances, otherwise known as the real world. It is about making good judgments that, in turn, enable us to make good choices.

Furthermore, it is worth noting that the fact that human beings are free rational beings has itself been an inspiration for a whole school of philosophical ethics known as personalism.[14] The idea is usually traced to the German philosopher Immanuel Kant, who wrote,

> The beings whose existence rests not on our will but on nature nevertheless have, if they are beings without reason, only a relative worth as means, and are called *things*; rational beings, by contrast, are called *persons*, because their nature already marks them out as ends in themselves, i.e., as something that may not be used merely as means, [and] hence to that extent limits all arbitrary choice (and is an object of respect).[15]

For Kant, human persons have equal and inviolable dignity and worth. We might call to mind the United States *Declaration of Independence*: "all men are created equal," and "they are endowed by their Creator with certain unalienable Rights."[16] According to Kant, they should not be used by others because they are rational beings capable of self-determination. In other words, they are made to be in control of their own lives. Similarly, Pope John Paul II spoke of "the primordial moral requirement of loving and respecting the person as an end and never as a mere means."[17]

If each person exists as an end in him or herself, then morally speaking one person cannot enslave another as a means to economic ends. One person cannot murder another to satisfy one's anger or jealousy. One cannot steal from another, using that person's possessions as if they were one's own. One cannot lie to another, deceiving that person into believing or doing one's own will when he or she otherwise would not. By this account, all immorality reduces persons to be used as unwilling means for others. All moral behavior treats others with the utmost dignity and "absolute worth."[18]

From this one principle, we can get about half of the Ten Commandments ("do not murder"; "do not steal"; "do not lie"; and so forth). Kant calls this simply the moral law. Other people call it natural law because it is a moral principle informed by our nature as rational beings made by God for virtue. Furthermore, we have a certain innate or natural knowledge of it. Our conscience testifies to it within us. Natural law is sometimes conceived as a broader moral category than Kant's principle, but his imperative is a good, basic rule of thumb so long as we remember our need for prudence in its application.

Now, reason has its limits too. As I have already hinted at, it allows us to discover all sorts of amazing things about the created order, about basic right and wrong, and about what is practical in any given moment and situation. But reason doesn't give us exhaustive knowledge about all sorts of things. Anyone who has tried to boil down a relationship to if-then scenarios in their heads knows that real people don't often follow formulas. We are "fearfully and wonderfully made," and that sometimes means that we're scary and unpredictable to each other. Our expectations of others—though not always without merit—can prove wrong for millions of reasons, mostly because of what we don't know and often can't know.

Another area where reason is limited is theology. I've said that God is rational, but it would be more accurate to say that God is supra-rational. That is, God is far more (*supra*)—but not less—than what we understand by rational. In fact, he is simply far more than we can understand, period.

The biblical story of Job seems to get at this. Job did everything right, but everything went wrong for him. He lost his children, his wife, and even his health. By his own logic, which was valid, he didn't deserve what had happened to him. It wasn't fair. Or, at least, he couldn't see how it could possibly be fair. Instead of offering Job an explanation or a formula to help him understand how everything he experienced actually made sense after all, God responds by reminding Job of how little he knows or can know:

Then the LORD answered Job out of the whirlwind, and said:

> "Who is this who darkens counsel
> By words without knowledge?
> Now prepare yourself like a man;
> I will question you, and you shall answer me.
>
> "Where were you when I laid the foundations
>   of the earth?
> Tell me, if you have understanding.
> Who determined its measurements?
> Surely you know!
> Or who stretched the line upon it?
> To what were its foundations fastened?
> Or who laid its cornerstone,
> When the morning stars sang together,
> And all the sons of God shouted for joy?"
>
> (Job 38:1–7)

God goes on like that for a while, hammering on the point that there are billions of things about him and the world that Job does not and cannot know or understand. At the same time, God does give Job greater knowledge of himself, a knowledge that goes beyond reasoned speculation: revelation. "I have heard of You by the hearing of the ear," says Job at the end, "But now my eye sees You" (Job 42:5).

In fact, many traditional divine attributes are actually just admissions of our ignorance. Immutable means "not changeable." Impassible means "not passionate." Infinite means "not limited." Good theology isn't so much about speculation as it is learning about God by admitting what we don't and can't know and instead opening our eyes to who he reveals himself to be. This is scary and unpredictable, but thankfully it is also hopeful and surprising. As St. Paul writes, referencing the prophet Isaiah, "Eye has not seen, nor ear heard, nor have entered into the heart of man the things which God has prepared for those who love Him" (1 Cor. 2:9). God is not only more than what we can know or reason or understand, he's unimaginably better.

Animals

It might seem odd to some to say that we are animals. At one time, it was more common in English to speak of nonhuman animals as *beasts*, which I suspect made the label "animal" less off-putting. But now beast is more often synonymous with *monster*, and we're left without a good word to distinguish between humans and nonhuman animals. In this light, I sometimes find it odd when people pass around internet memes about nonhuman animals grieving or pairing up or expressing emotion in a variety of other ways, as if it should amaze us, as if that made them nearly human. The instinct for sympathy is a good one. But the basis is off. That is, the opposite reality is true: our emotions, sensations, feelings, and everything else about our bodily lives are what make *us* animals.

Thus, it is traditional (and more importantly *true*) to say that human beings are not merely rational, but rational *animals*. We are neither disembodied spirits, like the angels, nor are we bodily but emotionless, like Vulcans from *Star Trek*. We are incarnate beings, and our lives are full of laughter, anger, joy, disappointment, celebration, weeping, boredom, excitement, pleasure, and all the rest. We share most of these in common with other animals, but such things are not, for that, less human. And, of course, human and beastly emotions are not exactly the same. In fact, as humans, we experience bodily life uniquely, as free, rational beings. As John Paul II put it, "reason and free will are linked with all the bodily and sense faculties."[19]

It is sometimes said that traditional Christian ethics and spirituality are all about the supremacy of reason over our passions. There is some truth to this, but it is too simplistic. Early Christians did not think that all emotion was bad. In fact, like the Stoics before them, they insisted that under the right conditions human passions, precisely because they are human, can be good, moral, and even rational.

Saint Augustine certainly believed this when he prayed, "O Lord ... our heart is restless until it rests in thee."[20] Desire plays a prominent role in many of his works, in fact. Either our desire is first of all moved by love of God and we find the peace we need to rightly love everything else, or we desire other things more than God out of a twisted, disordered love that leaves us empty. To the extent that this passion is put to good use—loving God first, then people, then the world—it is moral and rational. In fact, it is of great assistance to us. Strong passion can keep us dedicated and faithful to our hopes, dreams, ideals, and values. It can push us to find a reasonable solution to a problem we are determined to solve. It can keep us focused on what is right and best in the midst of an imperfect and broken world. It can prompt us to do the right thing when we don't have the time to reflect and think over every option. And it can guide us with instincts and intuitions that are important and true of their own right. As the French philosopher Blaise Pascal put it, "The heart has its reasons which reason itself does not know."[21]

Similarly, our bodies are an essential part of who we are, and they, too, can reflect the image of God. The body is the instrument of the soul. We do not act, except bodily. Even our thinking, modern neuroscience has shown, is not a totally disembodied activity—our brains are full of activity when we use our minds to think. Thus, we cannot do what is right and rational and moral, except bodily. Not in this world anyway. And our bodily life can itself be of great assistance to growing in the likeness of God. In fact, our bodies are so essential to who we are that, from the beginning, Christians (and others) have firmly believed in the idea of resurrection, that someday the unnatural separation of soul and body that happens in death will be set right by God once again.

Highlighting the importance of our embodied realities and following Jesus's Sermon on the Mount (Matt. 5–7), spiritual practices have taken a central place in the Christian life. Jesus taught his followers not only to pray but to pray simply, quietly, together corporately, and secretly in solitude. Many passages in the Bible stress our posture as well: standing, raising our hands, kneeling, lying prostrate. Jesus also taught his disciples to fast in such a way that they wouldn't make a show and draw attention to themselves. He taught them to give alms or charity in the same way and to be satisfied with simplicity. And so on. All of these have an essentially bodily component to them. Christian asceticism does not view the body as evil. Quite the opposite, in fact.

According to St. Moses the Ethiopian, a fourth-century monk of the Egyptian desert, these disciplines should be "rungs of a ladder up which [the heart] may climb to perfect charity [i.e., love]."[22] They teach us not to be idealists. And they also teach us how not to be, as C. S. Lewis put it, "men without chests"— people who out of hubris think that reason alone can solve every problem and gain mastery even over our own nature.[23] The point of this spirituality, by contrast, is to put all our thoughts and feelings in order, to push away, by developing good habits, everything that distracts us from that love that "God is" (1 John 4:8). In that sense, it is similar to how God pushed away all of Job's misconceptions in order to reveal himself to him. Thus, we can say that our freedom, creativity, reason, emotions, passions, feelings, appetites, and desires can all be put to good use, through daily discipline that involves the whole person, body and soul, *if and only if* they are tempered by humility.

So our passions, feelings, appetites, and sensations can be good as well. They are an essential part of our humanity. We would not be better off without them. In fact, we would not even be whole human beings without them. But they have their limits too. Feelings can be fickle and fleeting. On their own, they are not a firm foundation for moral or meaningful judgment. To say, "I *feel* like X is true or right," tells us nothing about whether X actually is so. It only tells us about our perception of X. That perception may be accurate. As I have already said, our passions and feelings can be of great moral and spiritual assistance to us. But they are no excuse for checking reason, freedom, or virtue at the door. They are necessary but not sufficient.

The American philosopher Robert Nozick offers a particularly compelling thought experiment for why mere experience— whether sensual, emotional, or intellectual—is not enough for us:

> Suppose there were an experience machine that would give you any experience you desired. Superduper neuro-psychologists could stimulate your brain so that you would think and feel you were writing a great novel, or making a friend, or reading an interesting book. All the time you would be floating in a tank, with electrodes attached to your brain. Should you plug into this machine for life, preprogramming your life's experiences?[24]

He even stipulates, "while in the tank you won't know that you're there; you'll think it's all actually happening."[25] What do you think? Most people instinctively recoil from this idea. I wonder if the Wachowski brothers had Nozick's experience machine in mind when they created *The Matrix* film series. The whole point of those widely popular movies was *getting out* of the machine because imagining being plugged into the Matrix generally creeps us out.

Nozick thinks there are good reasons for this common reaction. He offers three in particular:

1. First, we want to *do* certain things, and not just have the experiences of doing them.

2. A second reason for not plugging in is that we want to *be* a certain way, to be a certain sort of person. Someone floating in a tank is an indeterminate blob. There is no answer to the question of what a person is like who has long been in the tank. Is he courageous, kind, intelligent, witty, loving? It's not merely that it's difficult to tell; there is no way he is.

3. Third, plugging into an experience machine limits us to a man-made reality, to a world no deeper or more important than that which people can construct. There is no *actual* contact with any deeper reality, though the experience of it can be simulated.[26]

From what we have already said, we could summarize this by saying that mere experience is not enough because, deep down, we know that we were made (1) to do actual things of our own accord (i.e., freely), (2) to be virtuous, and (3) to explore and delight in God's world. Nozick even suggests that nonhuman animals might at least want or deserve (1) and (3) as well.

Thus, our bodily, animal life has its own limits, just like our freedom and rationality. But as it turns out, there is another, darker limit that applies to all of the elements of our humanity.

Corrupted by Sin and Death

It turns out we're not good at being humble or moral or loving. In fact, it even seems much harder than it ought to be. As St. Paul put it, "the good that I will to do, I do not do; but the evil I will not to do, that I practice" (Rom. 7:19). What gives? Why is knowing and wanting and trying to do the right thing still not enough for us?

The Judeo-Christian tradition has always added this further limitation to our humanity: we are corrupted by sin and death. We may be free, but often we are either weak-willed or we intentionally use our freedom in servitude to sin. We may be rational and creative, but as the Protestant Reformer John Calvin put it, "the human mind is, so to speak, a perpetual forge of idols."[27] Reason can be used to justify evil just as well as it can be used to discover what is good. Our passions and sensations may be capable of exalting our souls to new heights of virtue and love, but they just as often serve as the source of vice and hatred. We even have a concept of a "crime of passion," when in the heat of the moment a person's better judgment is overpowered by anger or fear or desperation.

Sin and evil are not themselves "things" but are a corruption of those things—such as freedom, reason, and passion—that God created to be good. So when we rebel against God's good order, we embrace emptiness and chaos. And because we are free, we are responsible for the corruption that we have wrought.

Moreover, as St. Paul remarked, "the wages of sin is death" (Rom. 6:23). Ecclesiastes elaborates on the tragic result. God created us in his image and "has put eternity in [our] hearts" (3:11), but "what happens to the sons of men also happens to animals; one thing befalls them: as one dies, so dies the other" (3:19). There is a certain futility or absurdity to our lives. We have inherited a world of heartbreak. Time has been transformed from a process of growth to one of decay. Not only do we die, but our hopes, dreams, friends, marriages, communities, concepts, ideas, experiences, and feelings are all mortal too. As we pass from one moment to the next, we are, in a sense, continually dying. In our current condition, as John Paul II put it, "the first absolutely certain truth of our life, beyond the fact that we exist, is the inevitability of our death."[28]

The fifth-century church father Pope St. Leo the Great frames our dilemma perfectly:

> when a man is changed by some process from one thing into another, not to be what he was is to him an ending, and to be what he was not is a beginning. But the question is, to what a man either dies or lives: because there is a death, which is the cause of living, and there is a life, which is the cause of dying.[29]

Left to ourselves, we find ourselves trapped in that "life, which is the cause of dying." We need help. We need the grace of divine love that alone is stronger than death. And we need humility to continually admit that. From a Christian point of view, that is where the gospel of Jesus Christ offers the answer. I cannot give a comprehensive theology of salvation here, so I will focus on one basic point. As Hebrews puts it, "Inasmuch then as the children have partaken of flesh and blood, [Jesus] Himself likewise shared in the same, that through death He might destroy him who had the power of death, that is, the devil, and release those who through fear of death were all their lifetime subject to bondage" (2:14–15).

Christ shows us that the answer to death is not escape but resurrection. We need his resurrection first of all. But then in our own lives we need to deny ourselves, take up our own crosses daily, and follow him (see Luke 9:23). We cannot live a resurrected life without dying first. We cannot live righteously without dying to our former, sinful ways. As the German Lutheran theologian, pastor, and martyr Dietrich Bonhoeffer put it, "When Christ calls a man, he bids him come and die."[30] He continued,

> In fact every command of Jesus is a call to die, with all our affections and lusts. But we do not want to die, and therefore Jesus Christ and his call are necessarily our death as well as our life. The call to discipleship, the baptism in the name of Jesus Christ means both death and life.[31]

Unlike the death that through fear keeps us in bondage to sin, this costly grace is that "death, which is the cause of living." True progress in a world corrupted by sin and death means dying and rising daily to new life through faith in the power of the cross of Jesus Christ.

This grace is not opposed to our nature. In fact, not only does it restore us to how we were made, it is essential to realizing what we were created to become. As that giant of medieval theology, the Western saint Thomas Aquinas, put it, "grace does not destroy nature, but perfects it."[32] We've already spoken of the law of nature and its relation to the Ten Commandments, so we can see the biblical basis of this concept: "Do not think that I came to destroy the Law or the Prophets," says Jesus. "I did not come to destroy but to fulfill" (Matt. 5:17). So too with the natural law. God's world does not exist apart from his grace and love, and everything he has made finds its perfection and fulfillment in them through Jesus Christ ... even that goofy little joke we call the human race.

Discussion Questions

1. How would you personally answer the question: "What does it mean to be human?"
2. Is there anything you think the author overlooked or underemphasized?
3. Was there anything surprising about the author's definition of humanity?
4. How does your concept of God affect your understanding of being created in his image?
5. How does your understanding of human nature affect the way you live your life?

Notes

1. Gregory of Nyssa, *On the Making of Man*, 16.4 in *NPNF*[2] 5:403. Herein, *NPNF*[1] refers to *Nicene and Post-Nicene Fathers*, Series 1 and *NPNF*[2] refers to *Nicene and Post-Nicene Fathers*, Series 2, originally published by Eerdmans and now public domain and available online at the Christian Classics Ethereal Library (ccel.org). The number before the colon is the volume number. The number after the colon is the page number.

2. Mark Twain, *The Bible According to Mark Twain*, ed. Howard G. Beatzhold and Joseph B. McCullough (Athens: University of Georgia Press, 1995), 329.

3. Vladimir Solovyov, *The Justification of the Good*, trans. Natalie Dudington, ed. Boris Jakim (Grand Rapids: Eerdmans, 2005), 92.

4. John of Damascus, *An Exact Exposition of the Orthodox Faith*, 2.27 in *NPNF*[2] 9:40b.

5. Daniel Silliman, "You Are Spiritual But Not Religious: The Secret Spiritual History of the Choose Your Own Adventure Books," *Religion Dispatches*, April 21, 2015, http://religiondispatches.org/you-are-spiritual-but-not-religious-the-secret-spiritual-history-of-the-choose-your-own-adventure-books/.

6. John of Damascus, *An Exact Exposition*, 2.24, 38b.

7. John Emerich Edward Dalberg-Acton, "The Roman Question," *The Rambler* (January 1860): 146.

8. Benjamin Franklin, *Letter to Messrs, the Abbes Chalut, and Arnaud*, April 17, 1787, in Franklin, *The Works of Benjamin Franklin*, vol. 10 (Cambridge, MA: C. Tappan, 1844), 38.

9. John of Damascus, *An Exact Exposition*, 2.24, 39b.

10. Epictetus, *Discourses*, 2.17 in Epictetus, *The Discourses of Epictetus; with the Encheiridion and Fragments*, trans. George Long (London: George Bell and Sons, 1887), 155.

11. John of Damascus, *An Exact Exposition*, 2.28, 40b.

12. Abraham Kuyper, *Lectures on Calvinism* (Grand Rapids: Eerdmans, 1934), 114.

13. Peter L. Berger, *Invitation to Sociology: A Humanistic Perspective* (Garden City, NY: Anchor Books, 1963), 17.

14. For an accessible introduction, see Jonas Norgaard Mortensen, *The Common Good: An Introduction to Personalism* (Frederiksværk, Denmark: Boedal Publishing, 2014).

15. Immanuel Kant, *Groundwork for the Metaphysics of Morals*, trans. Allen W. Wood (New Haven and London: Yale University Press, 2002), 46.

16. United States Congress, *Declaration of Independence*, July 4, 1776, http://www.archives.gov/exhibits/charters/declaration_transcript.html.

17. John Paul II, Encyclical Letter *Veritatis Splendor*, August 6, 1998, http://w2.vatican.va/content/john-paul-ii/en/encyclicals/documents/hf_jp-ii_enc_06081993_veritatis-splendor.html, 48.

18. Kant, *Groundwork*, 46. This paragraph has been adapted from an essay I wrote. See Dylan Pahman, "An Ancient Kantian Defense of the Resurrection," *Ethika Politika*, November 4, 2013, https://ethika-politika.org/2013/11/04/ancient-kantian-defense-resurrection/.

19. John Paul II, *Veritatis Splendor*, 48.

20. Augustine of Hippo, *Confessions*, vol. 1, *Introduction and Text*, ed. James J. O'Donnell (Oxford: Oxford University Press, 1992), 3, my translation.

21. Blaise Pascal, *Pensées* in Pascal, *Pensées and Other Writings*, trans. Honor Levi (Oxford: Oxford University Press, 1995), 158.

22. John Cassian, *Conferences*, 1.7, in *Western Asceticism*, ed. Owen Chadwick (Philadelphia: Westminster Press, 1979), 198.

23. See C. S. Lewis, *The Abolition of Man* (New York: Harper and Brothers, 1944).

24. Robert Nozick, *Anarchy, State, Utopia* (New York: Basic Books, 1974), 42.

25. Nozick, *Anarchy, State, Utopia*, 43.

26. Nozick, *Anarchy, State, Utopia*, 43.

27. John Calvin, *Institutes of the Christian Religion*, trans. Henry Beveridge (Christian Translation Society, 1845), 1.11.8, 97.

28. John Paul II, Encyclical Letter *Fides et Ratio*, September 14, 1998, http://w2.vatican.va/content/john-paul-ii/en/encyclicals/documents/hf_jp-ii_enc_14091998_fides-et-ratio.html, 26.

29. Leo the Great, *Sermons*, 71, in *NPNF*[2] 12:182.

30. Dietrich Bonhoeffer, *The Cost of Discipleship*, trans. R. H. Fuller (New York: Touchstone, 1995), 89.

31. Bonhoeffer, *The Cost of Discipleship*, 90.

32. Thomas Aquinas, *Summa Theologica*, Ia q. 1 a. 8 ad. 2 in Aquinas, *Summa Theologica: First Complete American Edition*, vol. 1, trans. Fathers of the English Dominican Province (New York: Benziger Brothers, 1948), 6.

2

What Is Society?

*Deprive a man of what he owes to others, beginning
with his parents and ending with the state and
world-history, and nothing will be left of his
existence, let alone his freedom. It would be madness
to deny this fact of inevitable dependence.*

—Vladimir Solovyov [1]

Introduction

In the previous chapter, we covered some ground regarding *individual* human persons. But no one exists apart from others. And other people constantly challenge us to go beyond our own concepts and comforts. It's a bit annoying, to be honest.

In the real world, all that high-sounding talk about human dignity doesn't always appear to correspond to our daily reality of life with others. As a general rule, most people tend toward some form of nerdery, some weird little obsession—such as sports, video games, philosophy, music, or literature. Or else they at least tend to have some personal (usually minor) neurosis, like an aversion to a certain smell or fear of spiders or always having to have the last word. Some people have more than others. The point is that real, flesh-and-blood human persons do not evoke our respect as naturally as an abstract treatise on human dignity might imply.

I am reminded of one *Peanuts* comic in which Linus shouts, "*I love mankind ... it's people* I can't stand!!" And, frankly, Linus is right, even if he overstates his case. It is a common if not essential feature of human personhood that any given person, with enough exposure, will grow *annoying* to our unsanctified hearts. How did we ever get stuck with these ... *people* anyway?[2]

For starters, we can look again at Genesis. The first chapter matter-of-factly states, "God created man in His own image; in the image of God He created him; male and female He created them" (Gen. 1:27). Male and female—God created us differently from the beginning. As for why, the best we get is the following: "Then God blessed them, and God said to them, 'Be fruitful and multiply; fill the earth and subdue it'" (Gen. 1:28). So the reason for the sexes is ... well ... sex. But that doesn't really answer our question. Why reproduce in the first place? Why would we want more people? Certainly "because God told us to" is a good reason (one among many), but he also made us rational creatures. As Aristotle put it, "All men by nature desire to know."[3]

To satisfy that desire, Genesis 2 offers a further explanation that comes right after the six days of creation in Genesis 1. One constant refrain there, as we have already examined, was "And God saw that [X] was good." So in Genesis 2, we ought to take notice when God, after creating a man from the dust of the earth, adds the word *not*. In particular, he says, "It is not good *that man should be alone*" (Gen. 2:18). As the moral philosopher and classical economist Adam Smith put it, "Man naturally desires, not only to be loved, but to be lovely; or to be that thing [that] is the natural and proper object of love."[4] And we can't do that without each other.

The story in Genesis continues to say that first God makes all the animals and brings them to the man, "But for Adam [Hebrew for 'human'] there was not found a helper comparable to him" (Gen. 2:20). Animals are great companions, and I think domesticating animals is a beautiful way of passing on some of God's image (self-control, virtue, reason) beyond our own species, but our pets are not "comparable" to us. They are not of the same nature or of equal dignity. So after the man meets and names all the animals and still feels alone, God finally makes woman.

When Adam first sees Eve, he exclaims, "This at last is bone of my bones and flesh of my flesh" (Gen. 2:23 RSV). At last!—someone like me. At last!—another human person. With a sigh of relief, he says, "Now, finally, I won't be lonely anymore." Furthermore, the text states, "Therefore a man leaves his father and his mother and cleaves to his wife, and they become one flesh" (2:24). One way of understanding this text is that it is the story of the creation of the family, the most basic social institution. It is the nature of the family to be the place where we first encounter other people, and that encounter is meant to be open, accepting, and without pretense: "And the man and his wife were both naked, and were not ashamed" (2:25).

We know already, however, that such ideals are not the reality that we currently live in. This first family, according to Genesis 4, is torn apart by shame, insecurity, and envy when their eldest son Cain kills his younger brother Abel. The Bible is full of stories of broken families, in fact. The genealogy of Jesus (see Matthew 1 or Luke 3) includes some of the most dysfunctional families that can be imagined. Family is a beautiful institution, and at its best, it is a place of love, encouragement, discipline, and sacrifice, where human persons can find true relief from their loneliness. But when it's broken, it can amplify, rather than satisfy, that unfulfilled desire to love and to be loved.

In addition, each of us needs to be and is meant to be "a helper" to one another in our own particular capacities. Again, we are meant to build one another up, and the family is the place where the foundation of our lives is established. While the family is unique (and it can be an error to extend the metaphor too far), we can see in the family a seed of all other forms of human community as well. Healthy families have an authority structure: the parents are in charge, not the children. Healthy families have good rules: such as "no hitting your sister" or "do your chores, then you can play video games." Healthy families require self-sacrifice: the parents work to provide for the children; the children obey and contribute their own labor to the maintenance of the household. We can even say that healthy families are ascetic:

they share meals together according to their own dietary rules, such as "no ice cream until dessert." They pray together. They spend intentional time together. Healthy families are also self-ruling and self-determining—that is—free. Their neighbors don't need to call the cops on them, for example.

We can see here several essential elements of society: freedom, authority, law, and self-restraint. In this way, the family is also our essential training ground for every other human community to which we will belong. With this in mind, we can offer the following preliminary answer to this chapter's question: society is *human persons in communities, within spheres, under just laws, for the common good.* The rest of this chapter will break down this definition and examine each element.

Persons in Communities

A person is not merely an individual, detached from all other people in the world. Persons are essentially connected to one another. We are social. But does that mean that we are not individuals at all? Are we just drops in the great sea of society, faceless masses whose component parts (individuals) are exchangeable and replaceable?

We have a ready answer to this: To the extent that persons are free, rational beings, they are self-determining and cannot morally be reduced to means for other ends, whether they be the ends of one, many, or all. To do such a thing is dehumanizing. Each person has inherent dignity and cannot be thought of as replaceable. Of course, we are all differently talented. And for any particular task, many people may be equally qualified—I do not mean to deny that kind of functional replaceability. But the unique life, personality, and gifts of each person are irreplaceable and priceless. We may think of St. Paul's reflection on the church as the body of Christ:

> If the foot should say, "Because I am not a hand, I am not of the body," is it therefore not of the body? And if the ear should say, "Because I am not an eye, I am not of the body," is it therefore not of the body? If the whole body were an eye, where would be the hearing? If the whole were hearing, where would be the smelling? But now God has set

the members, each one of them, in the body just as He pleased. And if they were all one member, where would the body be? (1 Cor. 12:15–19)

Of course, what is said about the church does not always apply to every other human community. But certainly everyone has an essential place in society as a whole. Our differences and diversity can be great assets, even if we often corrupt them into sources of strife.

Yet to say that human persons are essentially related to others does not mean that they are reducible to their social relations. That was Karl Marx's perspective, and he was wrong. Friedrich Engels, Marx's lifelong intellectual partner, even took this notion to its logical end, unironically claiming,

> While Marx discovered the materialist conception of history, Thierry, Mignet, Guizot and all the English historians up to 1850 are evidence that it was being striven for, and the discovery of the same conception by Morgan proves that the time was ripe for it and that it simply *had* to be discovered.[5]

If there had been no Marx, someone else would have done it, Engels claims. That is, even Marx himself was simply the replaceable byproduct of the social dialectic he claimed to have discovered! To be sure, our lives are profoundly affected by our relationships and material circumstances, but neither we nor the workings of history are *determined* by them. We are free. Each individual has his or her own road of life and his or her own choices to make along the way, even Karl Marx. Otherwise, we could not hold people responsible for their poor choices or honor them for their good ones.

That said, we need to ask the opposite question: Is society merely an aggregate of individual persons? Does it have any reality itself? Many would say no. This is a less harmful error; it doesn't require treating persons as mere means to the ends of any social whole, but it is still mistaken. It ultimately denies that there really is a social whole and thus implicitly denies that there can actually be any such thing as the common good, social responsibility, communion, or community. Every community or society, from this point of view, is just an aggregate of individual experiences and actions.

Peter Berger gives us a better starting point:

> The sociologist thinks of "society" as denoting a large complex of human relationships, or to put it in more technical language, as referring to a system of interaction. The word "large" is difficult to specify quantitatively in this context.... Two people chatting on a street corner will hardly constitute a "society," but three people stranded on an island certainly will.

He continues on to say that the term "applies when a complex of relationships is sufficiently succinct to be analyzed by itself, *understood as an autonomous entity*, set against others of the same kind."[6] Basically, according to Berger, the sociologist sees a society as a group of people with a relationship that deserves study as an entity in its own right.

We can add to this a more philosophical and spiritual dimension by turning to the Russian Orthodox social philosopher S. L. Frank.

> [T]he frequent meetings of two persons and their mutual sympathy are not yet a union of friendship. Such a union exists when persons are *conscious* of each other as "friends," i.e., when they subordinate their relations to the *ideal of friendship*, when friendship as a "union," as a "unity," is apprehended by them as an objective principle that rules both of them.[7]

Frank sounds a bit too much like Plato in this passage, as if such ideals existed completely apart from their members. He clarifies a bit later, however, that such an ideal "is created by people themselves, grows out of their communal and collective life, and is rooted in this life; for this reason, it lives in time, is born, exists for a while, and disappears like all other life on earth." Thus, he emphasizes that "social phenomena depend on the human consciousness not only in their origin but also in their subsequent being."[8] This does not make our societies any more unreal than us as individuals, however. We, too, are temporal beings.

What Frank helps us see is how we can talk about societies without simply meaning an aggregate of individuals, and he is right to the extent that we simply become conscious of these realities in our day-to-day lives. However, his emphasis on consciousness could be misunderstood to mean that only those societies that are consciously *designed* have reality. But that's not what he's saying. All sorts of societies come about spontaneously, in the sense of originating without conscious planning or sometimes as a different result than what had been planned, and Frank certainly knew that. For example, he wrote, "The leaders of the French Revolution desired to attain liberty, equality, fraternity, and the kingdom of truth and reason, but they actually created a bourgeois order. And this is the way it usually is in history."[9]

What might be more problematic is Frank's insistence that societies have no existence *apart from* the consciousness of their members. I think this somewhat confuses epistemology with ontology. That is, the way we come to know something does not necessarily tell us precisely what that thing is. Let's consider Frank's example of friendship again. Is it true that a friendship does not exist until the friends are conscious of it? Isn't it more often the case that people become conscious of what has already been a reality? The answer lies somewhere after "two persons and their mutual sympathy" but *before* they become conscious of their friendship. Indeed, what they become conscious of is that they have *already* "subordinate[d] their relations to the *ideal of friendship*." To realize, "Sally and I are friends," certainly cannot mean that we weren't actually friends until that particular moment.

So when we talk about persons in communities, spheres, societies, or simply society in the singular, we do not mean a mere aggregate of individual persons nor a big blob that consumes all individuality. The Protestant reformer Johannes Althusius summed up this idea well:

> Even though the individual persons of a community may
> be changed by the withdrawal or death of some superiors
> and inferiors, the community itself remains. It is held to

> be immortal because of the continued substitution and suc-
> cession of men in place of those withdrawing. Whence it
> appears that the community is different from the individual
> persons of a community, although it is often considered to
> be a representational and fictional person.

He earlier qualifies this by saying that the community "may be continuous and *almost* immortal," which fits with Frank's emphasis on temporality better.[10] Otherwise his take is pretty good. One might further object that we've arrived back at the idea of replaceable persons again when he talks about "the continued substitution and succession of men," but he doesn't mean that the persons are of *incidental* value and in that sense replaceable. Rather, he is simply pointing out that communities often continue beyond the lives of their members. They are more than mere aggregates.

Sports offer a multitude of examples in this regard. We root for our favorite teams, despite the fact that from season to season, and often even midseason, the players are exchanged and replaced. We talk about team records and histories. And we also talk about how the team was at its best or worst when Johnny Football Hero was on the team or coaching and so on. Or we talk about the '85 Bears or the '89 Pistons. The members are not incidental at all, but the teams are more than the players and staff.

Furthermore, we expect these human communities to be free, rational, passionate, and bodily. How often do we lament: "The refs are unfair!" or "What a stupid play call!" or "They just don't have heart this year" or "Too many injuries forced us to rely on weaker players"? Rather, it is when all of these things so essential to our humanity come together that we have a good team. Actually, that's not quite everything. Good teams also need virtue: penalties, cheating, and scandals can hurt the most autonomous teams with the best strategies, the most passion, and the fittest players.

In summary, Wolfgang Grassl, a Roman Catholic philosopher and professor of business administration at St. Norbert College, put it best: "a society composed of human persons is also a whole composed of wholes rather than of [mere] individuals."[11] Too often, people put the emphasis just on one or the other. The idea of personhood, however, includes our relationships and thus our societies and communities. These are organic realities of wholes consisting of wholes. One is not a mere component of the other. To this extent, we may speak of communities and larger groups having their own natures and purposes, whether consciously designed or spontaneously emerging from a human point of view. As we will see, human persons and communities are interdependent, often more so than we realize, which brings me to the idea of spheres.

Within Spheres

So what is a sphere anyway? I always need to shake the geometric image out of my head, as if social spheres were somehow actually giant round globes. That's definitely not what people mean by spheres in this context. Rather, social spheres are all the distinct domains of life, more general than, and inclusive of, particular communities. As domains, they have (or ought to have) their own sovereignty, freedom, authority, and power.

The Dutch Calvinist *Übermensch* Abraham Kuyper argued for a theological basis to this idea of sphere sovereignty (a term he actually coined). Kuyper wrote that "original, absolute sovereignty cannot reside in any creature but *must* coincide with God's majesty." For a biblical basis, he appealed to Jesus's words at his ascension: "All authority in heaven and on earth has been given to me" (Matt. 28:18 RSV). Kuyper continued to say that "an earthly sovereign possess[es] the power to compel obedience only in a limited sphere, a sphere bordered by other spheres in which another is sovereign and not he."[12] By contrast, only Jesus Christ has absolute sovereignty: "there is not a square inch in the whole domain of our human existence over which Christ, who is Sovereign over *all*, does not cry: 'Mine!'"[13]

The phrase "a sphere bordered by other spheres" makes me think of the ball pit at Chuck-E-Cheese's, which again is the wrong image. Both ball pits and sphere sovereignty are great ideas though. Kuyper's point is that only God has absolute power, and of course as a Christian he believed Jesus Christ to be both Lord and God. Another way of putting this is simply to say that no other human person is divine, and thus no merely human person can be trusted with absolute sovereignty. That's an idea even an atheist could get behind. Kuyper then applies it to society, claiming that all human authority is thus conditional, subject to a higher standard by which it can be judged and limited in its domain by the sovereignty of other spheres. In this way, while we may speak of religion as a sphere of social life when considered as an institution, S. L. Frank is right to stipulate, "In reality, however, the 'religious' life of a Christian is not some particular sphere of his life and activity, but *his very being.*"[14] As we are free beings subject to a transcendent order, so should our societies be. As we are responsible beings, so should those who exercise authority be held responsible.

Kuyper's conviction is echoed by Acton, who famously wrote to the Anglican bishop Mandell Creighton,

> I cannot accept your canon that we are to judge Pope and King unlike other men, with a favourable presumption that they did no wrong. If there is any presumption it is the other way against holders of power, increasing as the power increases. Historic responsibility has to make up for the want of legal responsibility. Power tends to corrupt and absolute power corrupts absolutely. Great men are almost always bad men, even when they exercise influence and not authority: still more when you superadd the tendency or the certainty of corruption by authority. There is no worse heresy than that the office sanctifies the holder of it.[15]

According to Acton, the historian has a moral duty not to gloss over the failures of past figures. no matter how great their reputations may be. Historians must hold responsible those who abused power with impunity in their own times. In the present, the way to mitigate the corrupting tendency of power and the temptation to use one's power to violate the rights of others is to set clear limits to power throughout society. Another way to say that is that Acton's solution to this problem is liberty.

Liberty is Kuyper's preferred solution as well. Neither of them were anarchists, however. In fact, both worked in government. Their conviction, rather, was that good government could not possess absolute sovereignty or power. Rather, each sphere, community, and person ought to be free to have its own limited sovereignty and power as well. For Kuyper, this meant that each has a calling before God, and each has its own contribution to make to the common good. Science, art, politics, commerce, religion, education, family, and whatever other sphere there may be or that may emerge according to God's timing and plan for the world have their own purpose or nature, and all of these ought to contribute freely to the good of others, especially the marginalized, as a matter of social solidarity.

Particular communities may fit into a variety of these spheres. Just as Lassie is a dog, a mammal, and an animal, a collective of artists may be not only an example of the sphere of art but also of commerce, friendship, financial support, and so on. As Kuyper himself put it, "no piece of our mental world is to be hermetically sealed off from the rest."[16] Another way to put it is that while the borders of each sphere should be clearly defined and protected, they are also *open* borders. We do not live our lives at one moment as a son or brother or father, then as a worker at another time, and then a citizen at yet another. Rather, we are simultaneously members of our families, jobs, nations, religions, and all other vocations of life.

We can't collapse any of these spheres into one another, either. Each realm of life has its own purpose and requires people uniquely competent to fulfill them. It is a corruption to run the state like a family business, unjustly favoring those related to public officials: that's what we call nepotism. It is a corruption to think of one's family in merely economic terms: family is a commitment greater than a contract and held together by familial and sacrificial love, which is a greater bond than the sympathy and mutual interest of economic exchange. As John Paul II put it, "it is preferable that each power be balanced by other powers and by other spheres of responsibility which keep it within proper bounds."[17]

This idea is akin to an application of the United States' founding fathers' notion of checks and balances, except throughout all society and not just in politics. As James Madison wrote,

> In order to lay a due foundation for that separate and
> distinct exercise of the different powers of government,
> which to a certain extent is admitted on all hands to be

essential to the preservation of liberty, it is evident that
each department should have a will of its own.[18]

Similarly, it is "essential to the preservation of liberty" that
each sphere of society and any community within it "should have
a will of its own." In fact, this has historically been part of the
American tradition of free association. As the French diplomat
Alexis de Tocqueville observed in the 1830s,

> The political associations which exist in the United States
> are only a single feature in the midst of the immense
> assemblage of associations in that country. Americans of
> all ages, all conditions, and all dispositions, constantly form
> associations. They have not only commercial and manu-
> facturing companies, in which all take part, but associa-
> tions of a thousand other kinds,—religious, moral, serious,
> futile, general or restricted, enormous or diminutive. The
> Americans make associations to give entertainments, to
> found seminaries, to build inns, to construct churches, to
> diffuse books, to send missionaries to the antipodes; they
> found in this manner hospitals, prisons, and schools.[19]

He continued to say, "If men living in democratic countries ...
never acquired the habit of forming associations in ordinary
life, civilization itself would be endangered."[20] That is, everything would have to be done by the state, and then no sphere or
community would have its own sovereignty, its own freedom to
creatively solve the problems and create the wealth of social life.

By contrast, when each person, community, and sphere
respects the sovereignty and liberty of others and fulfills its
obligations to them, there is justice. But there cannot be justice
without law—to which I now turn.

Under Just Laws

Law is another way in which the life of a society or community
outlives its members. Long after the original members have come
and gone, laws that they established may remain and continue
to affect the lives of those who come after them so long as those
social institutions survive and the laws remain enforced and

unchanged. But "law" is actually a bit ambiguous. What is a law? What different kinds of law are there and how are they related?

Thomas Aquinas gives us a good place to start: "Law is a rule and measure of acts, whereby man is induced to act or is restrained from acting."[21] He continues to say that law is "an ordinance of reason for the common good, made by him who has care of the community, and promulgated."[22] Of the different types of law, for our purposes we will look at natural law, common law, and positive law. In the course of doing that, I will also briefly define commutative, legal, and distributive justice, as well as justice in general.

First, Aquinas's definition is probably most compelling for *positive laws*: the laws of human governments. Keep in mind that government is a general term here. A poker club, for example, technically has an informal government that makes laws, such as "all drinks must be placed on coasters." It places a restraint on the action of its members. Because it concerns the duties of group members to the group as a whole, this would be an example of a law concerned with *legal justice*. It is also reasonable and for the common good: otherwise the moisture from the drinks might get on the cards. In the case of a poker club, such laws are typically made democratically by everyone or monarchically by the host, the protection of whose property (the cards and the table) is in everyone's interest. We might also say it is aimed at what is called *commutative justice* because in that case it would concern a relationship between equals (members to other members, groups to other groups, and so on). If the group bought pizza out of a common fund, it would be a violation of *distributive justice* if each person was not offered an equal number of slices. Distributive justice regulates the duties of groups to their members concerning what is common among them by virtue of their group membership. And finally, the law must be promulgated. If Jim hasn't arrived yet when the law is made, he has to be told about it if the others expect him to abide by it.

Second, *common law* fits this scenario pretty well too, but it is inherently less obvious. Common law is all the implied and inherited customs, cultural mores, and traditions of any society. They may have the same purpose, but no one may actually know the original reason they came about any more. Let's say at Bill's house everyone knows that aces are wild. When asked why, Bill just says, "That's the way my dad always played." When asked why Bill's dad played that way, he doesn't really know. That doesn't mean that the law isn't "an ordinance of reason ... made by him who has care of the community"; it just means that in this case Bill's dad (or whoever he got the idea from, however far back the tradition goes) passed on a custom to Bill. He may not have had any formal office, like poker club commander-in-chief, but he still made the rule out of a reasonable concern for the common good. Maybe he thought it makes games more exciting or makes the action quicker. Who knows? The purpose and origin of common laws are often not apparent and perhaps not even discoverable. They may, like Pascal's reasons of the heart, have their own reasons that reason itself cannot ultimately know. But they are still rules "whereby man is induced to act or is restrained from acting." And, again, such laws will not have force unless everyone knows about them.

All human laws can be either good or bad, just or unjust. In this case, Aquinas's definition is more aimed at what constitutes a *good* law and not simply any law. Some laws are immoral and irrational. Such unjust laws create discord in society instead of order and lead to its breakdown, just as the "law of sin" (Rom. 7:23) within us disorders and corrupts our personal lives. And this can include any human law, whether positive law or common law. For example, in the case of racism, we may think of American slavery or Jim Crow. But racial bias can pervade laws and customs more subtly and even unintentionally as well.

By way of analogy, I once saw an internet meme with the label "Racist Camera." The image showed a photo of a person of East Asian descent smiling on the display of a digital camera, with the automatic message across the screen: "Did someone blink?" Of course, the camera wasn't actually racist and the programmers probably weren't either. But the fact that they did not consider the almond-shaped eyes of over a billion people in the world to fit with what would be normal, unintentionally impressed a racial bias into the system that they developed. The same can be true of systems of human law, and this is possible for any other form of bias as well.

Theologian and cultural commentator Anthony Bradley provides an example in his analysis of proposals to change minimum wage laws. Many offer emotional, religious, and moral appeals to raise minimum wages to excessively high levels. However, against the good intentions of these advocates, Bradley writes,

> Such an increase ultimately hurts teens and low-skilled minorities because minimum wage jobs are usually entry-level positions filled by employees with limited work experience and few job skills. When the government forces employers to pay their workers more than a job's productivity demands, employers, in order to stay in business, generally respond by hiring fewer hours of low-skilled labor.[23]

A change in the law, with the intention to help such workers, actually may have the opposite effect. As Bradley notes, it is a greater problem that minorities are over-represented as a portion of low-skilled and inexperienced workers in the first place: "Employees who become more productive by gaining experience and improving their education earn larger raises and salaries in the long term."[24] But changing the law would unintentionally put up another barrier to minority and teenage workers' gaining work experience, while doing nothing to increase their education levels. In fact, if more of them see their hours cut or they become unemployed, they will have less extra money to spend on education or other skill training.

Finally, *natural law*, as we have already discussed, is the moral order built into the world by God. God our creator and provider made a rational order, for our good and his glory, and he promulgates it to us through the voice of conscience within us. As the church father St. John Chrysostom put it, "when God formed man, he implanted within him from the beginning a natural law. And what then was this natural law? He gave utterance to conscience within us; and made the knowledge of good things, and of those which are the contrary, to be self-taught."[25]

While the natural law is firmly established by God and the standard of what is right or wrong, human laws are changeable and can themselves be mistaken. They are only good by their relative approximation to the natural law. For example, even though the abolition of slavery is ideal—and it took shamefully long for most human societies to finally do away with it—sometimes the most prudent political policy is to take small steps in the right direction, like Christian Rome did.[26] If the ideal is practically impossible in any given circumstance, gradual approach toward that ideal may still be possible and desirable and may lay the foundation for greater change in the future. In fact, it may be unreasonable to expect more than that.

Why is law so important? Well, first because it is everywhere. As already mentioned, there is no society without laws, even if only unwritten ones, including the family. Second, just societies are characterized by the rule of law—the principle that all people, whether rich or poor, politician or citizen, of any race, creed, sex, and so on, are equally subject to the law. The law, not any person or group of people, is the ultimate ruler of the land. When the rule of law is absent, there is tyranny. Thus, the rule of law is equally necessary for a society to be not only just but also free.

But is justice reducible to equality? Definitely not. Referring to Exodus 1:8–22, Vladimir Solovyov pointed out that

> when the Pharaoh issued a law commanding to put to death all the Jewish new-born babes, this law was certainly not unjust on account of the unequal treatment of the Jewish and Egyptian babes. And if the Pharaoh subsequently gave orders to put to death all new-born infants and not only the Jewish ones, no one would venture to call this new law just, although it would satisfy the demand for equality.

Thus, he concludes, "Equality, then, can be just or unjust."[27] The classic definition of justice is to give to each what is due. While different roles of life or levels of social organization may be due to different things, nothing exempts anyone or any group from the demands of justice. In this sense, there is an aspect of equality that is essential to justice: the equal respect for the rights and obligations that apply to all people on the basis of natural law, in their own particular circumstances.

Theologically speaking, even God is just. He does not act arbitrarily. He does only what is right. There are several passages in the New Testament in which God is consistently referred to as not being a respecter of persons (*prosopolempsia*, see Acts

10:34; Rom. 2:11; Eph. 6:9), and Christians are called to do justice in their own communities in the same way (James 2:1) by not favoring the rich over the poor, for example. From this follows Acton's resistance "to judge Pope and King unlike other men." While prudence may be the premier intellectual virtue, justice is the primary social virtue, regulating all of our relationships, whether to God, to others, to our societies, from our societies to us, or from us to the world. Without justice we cannot have a free society, and without the rule of law we cannot have justice.

For the Common Good

So we have some idea of what laws and justice are and what different types there are, but what are laws for? Aquinas said "the common good," which is a decent answer, but that term is ambiguous—like "social justice," which I take to be a synonym. It might mean different things to different people. Thus, I'll try to refine our own concept here.

The Second Vatican Council succinctly defined the Roman Catholic notion of the common good as "the sum of those conditions of social life which allow social groups and their individual members relatively thorough and ready access to their own fulfillment." It goes on to say that in our present era the common good "takes on an increasingly universal complexion and consequently involves rights and duties with respect to the whole human race." Among those conditions of social life that constitute the common good are

> everything necessary for leading a life truly human, such as food, clothing, and shelter; the right to choose a state of life freely and to found a family, the right to education, to employment, to a good reputation, to respect, to appropriate information, to activity in accord with the upright norm of one's own conscience, to protection of privacy and rightful freedom even in matters religious.

Above all, it emphasizes that "the disposition of [social] affairs is to be subordinate to the personal realm and not contrariwise."[28] It thus affirms what we have already said about not making persons mere means to the ends of society. Rightly understood,

the common good is that which allows human beings to flourish *in* any given society, whether that may be a state, business,
religious institution, family, sports team, or poker club. It is
for the good of individuals and societies together. As Vladimir
Solovyov put it, "subordination to society uplifts the individual"
and "the independence of the individual lends strength to the
social order."[29]

The Roman Catholic tradition has articulated this idea well
in the principle of subsidiarity. As Pope Pius XI wrote,

> The supreme authority of the State ought, therefore, to let
> subordinate groups handle matters and concerns of lesser
> importance, which would otherwise dissipate its efforts
> greatly. Thereby the State will more freely, powerfully,
> and effectively do all those things that belong to it alone
> because it alone can do them: directing, watching, urging,
> restraining, as occasion requires and necessity demands.
> Therefore, those in power should be sure that the more
> perfectly a graduated order is kept among the various
> associations, in observance of the principle of "subsidiary
> function," the stronger social authority and effectiveness
> will be the happier and more prosperous the condition of
> the State.[30]

In short, the idea of subsidiarity is that whenever another
institution of society can handle a problem or meet a need, higher
levels of authority should back away and let them do so. This
principle can be applied beyond the state to churches, businesses, schools, and any other sphere or community of society. It
expresses the paradox that the less the state or any other higher
authority needs to do, the more effective it can be in handling the
tasks that are proper to it. In this sense, we can consider the principle of subsidiarity as a sort of social asceticism: self-restraint
for the sake of the betterment of oneself and one's neighbor, but
applied to whole communities, societies, and spheres.

Subsidiarity also places a mandate on higher levels of social
order to help when lower levels prove to be inadequate, though
always with an eye to restoring lower communities to a position
in which they can serve human needs on their own again. We
cannot have free societies without virtuous citizens and mem-

bers. As the eighteenth-century Anglo-Irish statesman Edmund Burke put it,

> Society cannot exist, unless a controlling power upon will and appetite be placed somewhere; and the less of it there is within, the more there must be without. It is ordained in the eternal constitution of things, that men of intemperate minds cannot be free. Their passions forge their fetters.[31]

When such intemperance prevents a lower community of society from fulfilling its vocation, a higher order must step in. Additionally, sometimes the causes are not vice or intemperance but simply circumstantial. Either way, subsidiarity reflects the principle that grace perfects nature: help from above should not replace lower institutions but should build them up, just as God's grace does not violate our natures but helps us be what we were meant to be.

From a Christian perspective, then, this leads to the conclusion that religious liberty in particular is of paramount importance to the common good, as Vatican II also proclaimed. In fact, there is a long, if often neglected and distorted, Christian tradition of this. Saint Constantine, the first Christian emperor of Rome, declared in his (so-called) Edict of Milan that "to each one freedom is to be given to devote his mind to that religion which he may think adapted to himself, in order that the Deity may exhibit to us in all things his accustomed care and favor."[32]

Now, we could understand this pluralistically, in the sense that any religion is just as good as any other. To some degree, that may, in fact, be the way that Constantine meant it. He was the head of state in a religiously diverse society, after all. But we could also understand it as acknowledging that respecting religious freedom, importantly including for Christians, is in accord with how God made us as free, rational beings. As the second-century *Epistle to Diognetus* put it, God "willed to save man by persuasion, not by compulsion, for compulsion is not God's way of working."[33]

In religiously liberal societies, Christian churches are free to preach the gospel, and people are free to enter the life of grace through the sacraments. From there, as members of the body of Christ and each in his or her own vocations, Christians ought to be bearers of God's saving grace throughout his world, in every sphere, community, and institution of society. We thus add this subsidiary benefit, that where we all fail—and "all have sinned" (Rom. 3:23)—God's saving grace might permeate our societies and raise us up once again. As Jesus himself put it, "To what shall I liken the kingdom of God? It is like leaven, which a woman took and hid in three measures of meal till it was all leavened" (Luke 13:20–21). So also, citizens of that kingdom are meant to be leaven in all the kingdoms of the world. For it is only by analogy that we can speak of the subsidiary help between purely human institutions as grace. But when the church is free to be the church, then divine grace, beyond God's work of providence and personal miracles, can work through its members to display the power and salvation of God to the world ... despite whatever annoying little quirks any of us may have.

Discussion Questions

1. What is a person? How do our relationships affect who we are?

2. How many different communities do you participate in every day? What's your role or vocation in each one?

3. How do you relate the different spheres of your own life (family, religion, government, science, art, business, and so on) to one another? How are they connected? How are they distinct?

4. What makes a law just? Is there anything you think the author left out?

5. How do sin and death affect your social life? Where do you see opportunities for grace?

Notes

1. Vladimir Solovyov, *The Justification of the Good*, trans. Natalie Dudington, ed. Boris Jakim (Grand Rapids: Eerdmans, 2005), 373.

2. These first two paragraphs have been adapted from an essay I wrote. See Dylan Pahman, "Dignity: A Dinosaur," *Ethika Politika*, March 31, 2015, https://ethikapolitika.org/2015/03/31/dignity-a-dinosaur/.

3. Aristotle, *Metaphysics*, trans. W. D. Ross in *Aristotle, The Basic Works of Aristotle*, ed. Richard McKeon (New York: Random House, 1941), 1.1, 98c22, 689.

4. Adam Smith, *The Theory of Moral Sentiments*, new ed. (London: Henry G. Bohn, 1853), 166.

5. Friedrich Engels, "Letters on Historical Materialism," in *The Marx-Engels Reader*, ed. Robert C. Tucker, 2nd ed. (New York; London: Norton & Company, 1978), 768.

6. Peter L. Berger, *Invitation to Sociology* (Garden City, NY: Anchor Books, 1963), 26, emphasis mine.

7. S. L. Frank, *The Spiritual Foundations of Society*, trans. Boris Jakim (Athens: Ohio University Press, 1987), 78.

8. Frank, *Spiritual Foundations*, 79.

9. Frank, *Spiritual Foundations*, 37.

10. Johannes Althusius, *Politica: An Abridged Translation of Politics Methodically Set Forth and Illustrated with Sacred and Profane Examples*, ed. and trans. Fredrick S. Carney (Indianapolis: Liberty Fund, 1964), 41, emphasis mine.

11. Wolfgang Grassl, "Integral Human Development in Analytical Perspective: A Trinitarian Model," *Journal of Markets & Morality* 16, no. 1 (Spring 2013): 149–50.

12. Abraham Kuyper, "Sphere Sovereignty" in *Abraham Kuyper: A Centennial Reader*, ed. James D. Bratt (Grand Rapids: Eerdmans, 1998), 466.

13. Kuyper, "Sphere Sovereignty," 488.

14. S. L. Frank, *The Light Shineth in Darkness*, trans. Boris Jakim (Athens, OH: Ohio University Press, 1989), 144.

15. John Emerich Edward Dalberg-Acton, "Acton-Creighton Correspondence," in *Essays in the Study and Writing of History*, Selected Writings of Lord Acton, vol. 2, ed. J. Rufus Fears (Indianapolis: Liberty Fund, 1986), 383.

16. Kuyper, "Sphere Sovereignty," 488.

17. John Paul II, Encyclical Letter *Centesimus Annus*, May 1, 1991, 44, http://w2.vatican.va/content/john-paul-ii/en/encyclicals/documents/hf_jp-ii_enc_01051991_centesimus-annus.html.

18. James Madison, "No. 51: The Structure of the Government Must Furnish the Proper Checks and Balances Between the Different Departments," in *The Federalist Papers: A Collection of Essays Written in Favor of the New Constitution*, by Alexander Hamilton, James Madison, and John Jay (Mineola, NY: Dover Publications, 2014), 253.

19. Alexis de Tocqueville, *Democracy in America*, vol. 2, trans. Henry Reeve, 4th ed. (Cambridge: Sever and Francis, 1864), 129.

20. Tocqueville, *Democracy in America*, vol. 2, 131.

21. Thomas Aquinas, *Summa Theologica* in Aquinas, *Summa Theologica: First Complete American Edition*, vol. 2, trans. Fathers of the English Dominican Province (London: Burns Oats & Washbourne, 1920), Ia-IIæ q. 90 a. 1, 587.

22. Aquinas, *Summa Theologica*, in Aquinas, *Summa Theologica*, Ia-IIæ q. 90 a. 4, 590.

23. Anthony Bradley, *Black and Tired: Essays on Race, Politics, Culture, and International Development* (Eugene, OR: Wipf & Stock, 2011), 49.

24. Bradley, *Black and Tired*, 49.

25. John Chrysostom, *Homilies on the Statues*, 12.9 in *NPNF*[1] 9:421.

26. See Justinian, *Justinian's Institutes*, trans. Peter Birks and Grant McLeod with the Latin text of Paul Krueger (Ithaca, NY: Cornell University Press, 1987), 1.1.2 and 1.5.3, 37–41. The *Institutes* state that slavery is against natural law, admitting that all people are born free. However, it notes that slavery had been permitted by the laws of the nations (*jus gentium*). It then boasts about all the ways in which Roman law had been reformed to make manumission or emancipation of slaves easier compared to those of other nations. That did not make slavery any less of a violation of nature,

but one can still acknowledge the relative good of laws that made freedom easier to obtain, considering the imperfect context.

27. Vladimir Solovyov, *The Justification of the Good*, 388–89. Solovyov has his own peculiar definition of justice—mercy equally applied—but I cannot address it here.

28. Second Vatican Council, Pastoral Constitution *Guadium et Spes*, December 7, 1965, http://www.vatican.va/archive/hist_councils/ ii_vatican_council/documents/vat-ii_const_19651207_gaudium-et-spes_en.html, 26. The preceding part of this paragraph was adapted from an essay I wrote. See Dylan Pahman, "The Common Good of All," *Ethika Politika*, June 11, 2014, https://ethikapolitika. org/2014/06/11/common-good/.

29. Solovyov, *The Justification of the Good*, 180.

30. Pius XI, Encyclical Letter *Quadragesimo Anno*, May 15, 1931, 80, http://w2.vatican.va/content/pius-xi/en/encyclicals/documents/hf_p-xi_enc_19310515_quadragesimo-anno.html.

31. Edmund Burke, *Letter to a Member of the National Assembly in Answer to Some Objections to His Book on French Affairs* in *The Works of the Right Honourable Edmund Burke*, vol. 4 (London: John C. Nimmo, 1887), 52.

32. In Eusebius Pamphilius, *Church History,* 10.5 in *NPNF*[2] 1:379.

33. *Epistle to Diognetus*, 7.4, in *Early Christian Fathers*, vol. 1 of *The Library of Christian Classics*, trans. and ed. Cyril C. Richardson (Philadelphia: Westminster Press, 1953), 7.4, 219.

3

What Is an Economy?

Commerce penetrates the secret places of the world, approaches shores unseen, explores fearful wildernesses, and in tongues unknown and with barbaric peoples carries on the trade of mankind. The pursuit of commerce reconciles nations, calms wars, strengthens peace, and commutes the private good of individuals into the common benefit of all.

—Hugh of St. Victor[1]

Introduction

My father-in-law is known for his one-liner jokes. For example, he is fond of telling people, "Do you know that of all the people I've met, you're one of them?" Similarly, of all the annoying people in the world, economists are some of them. Why does Victor Claar, for example, have to burst everyone's bubble by telling us that fair trade coffee isn't really, well, fair?

Kidding aside, economists often unfairly get a bad rap. Economics is sometimes even referred to as the "dismal science," a term supposedly coined in response to the Rev. Thomas Robert Malthus, one of the classical economists, and his 1798 book *An Essay on the Principle of Population.* Sometimes it also has been used in reference to the "iron law of wages," attributed

to the jurist Ferdinand Lassalle and later to the classical economist David Ricardo. Without going into details, early theories
like these gave the impression to some that improving the conditions of the poor was impossible. Hence, economic science has
been called dismal.

In actuality, however, the term dismal science originally had
little to do with all that. Instead, it came from the fact that in
the early nineteenth century, economists, by and large, opposed
slavery because they believed all people to be equal and free by
nature. The satirist Thomas Carlyle coined the term in an 1849
essay he wrote arguing *in favor of* reintroducing slavery to the
West Indies:

> [T]his [idea] of declaring that Negro and White are *unre-
> lated, loose from one another, on a footing of perfect equal-
> ity, and subject to no law but that of Supply and Demand
> according to the Dismal Science ... contradicts the pal-
> pable facts.[2]

What were those palpable facts to Carlyle? He claimed to
not want *real* slavery, of course, just lifetime forced servitude,
remarkably blind to the fact that there is no difference between
the two. Actually, he didn't even entirely rule out the former:

> You are not "slaves" now; nor do I wish, if it can be avoided,
> to see you slaves again, but decidedly you will have to be
> servants to those that are born *wiser* than you, that are
> born lords of you,—servants to the whites, if they *are* (as
> what mortal can doubt they are?) born wiser than you.[3]

Talk about dismal! Thankfully, Carlyle's views went unheeded.
Indeed, even the editors of the journal that published the essay
disavowed them, adding the following remark as part of a short
preface: "we have published the Article, at a cheap market-rate;
and give it publicity, without in the least committing ourselves
to the strange doctrines shadowed forth in it. Doctrines and
notions which, we rather suspect, are pretty much a 'minority
of one,' in the present era of the world!"[4]

The one thing Carlyle managed to do was coin a pejorative
term commonly used to stigmatize a whole new emerging branch
of science. Considering its origin—defense of human freedom

and equality and opposition to slavery—we might rather recall Christ's beatitude: "Blessed are those who are persecuted for righteousness' sake, for theirs is the kingdom of heaven" (Matt. 5:10). Sure, not all classical economists were pious Christians, and their work is not beyond criticism, but shouldn't we at least give credit where it's due?

I hope that this chapter might both demystify and similarly destigmatize some basic economic principles and business practices that have unjustly acquired bad reputations of their own. For example, sometimes economists use terms that ordinary people might use for other purposes. It's like they have their own language, which I will lovingly refer to as "Economish." If an outsider doesn't take the time to learn the language, they will not understand what the natives (economists) are talking about. So I'll translate where necessary. However, I should be clear that this chapter is not meant to be any sort of comprehensive introduction to economics, nor are those chapters that follow. Rather, this chapter continues our exploration of Christian anthropology and social thought by narrowing in on the economic aspect of our lives.

What is an economy? And what does it have to do with our faith?

Let's start again with Genesis. We are created in the image of God, who himself is creative, free, and rational. We are also part of creation and thus temporal, animal, and material. And we are created for each other to love and to be loved and to help one another. All of this, unfortunately, has been corrupted by sin and death. But all of this can still find its fulfillment through divine grace. What's missing from this picture? Economics!

After creating us in his image, God says, "Be fruitful and multiply; fill the earth and subdue it; have dominion over the fish of the sea, over the birds of the air, and over every living thing that moves on the earth" (Gen. 1:28). Creation isn't here just for us to look at. We have a vital role to play in God's purpose for the world. Genesis even says that after making Adam, "the LORD God took the man and put him in the garden of Eden to tend and keep it" (Gen. 2:15). We are meant "to till the ground" (2:5) of God's creation, the same ground from which we were made, and thereby to "be fruitful."

In short, God wants us to work. He wants us to creatively make good and beautiful things, just like he did (and does). There are similarities between Genesis and some other ancient Near Eastern stories in which people are also created to work. Unlike those stories, however, in Genesis people are made to be free, not to be slaves. God tells them to "have dominion," to take charge. Our work is meant to reflect his work, which also means that work is not all there is to life.

> Six days you shall labor and do all your work, but the seventh day is the Sabbath of the LORD your God.... For in six days the LORD made the heavens and the earth, the sea, and all that is in them, and rested the seventh day. (Ex. 20:9–11)

People disagree about how exactly to fulfill this command today, but the principle seems clear enough: Life is economic; economics is not all of life.

There is something else to this as well. In Genesis 1, God tells humanity, "See, I have given you every herb that yields seed which is on the face of all the earth, and every tree whose fruit yields seed; to you it shall be for food" (1:29). In Genesis 2, God tells Adam, "Of every tree of the garden you may freely eat" (2:16), adding only that one exception: "but of the tree of the knowledge of good and evil you shall not eat, for in the day that you eat of it you shall surely die" (2:17). Clearly we messed that up. The Hebrew idiom for "you shall surely die" could be literally translated, "dying, you shall die," underscoring, as we have already discussed, how in all of our days and not just our last we "walk through the valley of the shadow of death" (Ps. 23:4).

Nevertheless, we shouldn't overlook the other stuff: God gave us the world for our provision. He wants us to consume it (Economish for "use it") in a way that gives life ("for food"). He wants us to cooperate with him in the beautification and beatification of the cosmos. He blesses us so that we can be a blessing to the world and, in turn, to him. He could have done it himself by snapping his fingers (metaphorically, of course) and making a fully formed world. Instead, he made one that develops and grows over ages and ages. And he made us to take part in that, enjoy it, and spread his image over all creation.

So, what is an economy? For our purposes, we'll explore the following definition: an economy is *the cultivation of creation, through human labor, for the provision of human needs, through relationships of exchange.* As with our personal and social lives, so also our economic lives are not free from corruption by sin and death but are also in need of grace.

The Cultivation of Creation

The first thing we need for the cultivation of creation is some idea of property—the supply side of supply and demand. If no one can agree on who has the right to cultivate any given resource, cultivation will not happen. This is true of every economy in human history. All sorts of arrangements have been tried. One person or group of people might own everything and then give other people permission to cultivate their resources. Many people might own resources and cultivate those resources themselves. But without some concept of property, there is no cultivation.

This is so fundamental to our lives that God made it one of the Ten Commandments: "You shall not steal" (Ex. 20:15). Without property, this command would make no sense. It tells us that there is such a thing as property concerning which people have rights, limitations, and responsibilities. Societies without well-defined property rights in their laws open themselves to widespread theft and corruption by failing to properly account for this reality.

However, it would be a mistake to end the insight there. God may have made us to cultivate the world, but it is still *his* world, not ours. "The earth is the LORD's, and all that is in it," wrote the psalmist, "the world, and those who live in it" (Ps. 24:1 NRSV). As Abraham Kuyper put it, just as "God Almighty is the *Sovereign over all people*," so also "the same God Almighty is also the owner *of all property*."[5] The point is that human ownership must be subject to God. Morally speaking, we don't get to do whatever we want with our property. Instead, for the common good and the kingdom of God, we are stewards of a world that does not belong to us, and that includes the little pieces of that world that we own.

From this, Kuyper even expresses the conviction that with regard to animals, for example, "they have rights over man insofar as God has grounded those rights in their nature."[6] God has made each thing "according to its kind," and it is both immoral and irrational to treat those things otherwise. Animals are not crops. Plants are not rocks. Nevertheless, Kuyper is also quick to emphasize that it is "revolting to see how animals are given royal treatment while people are allowed to die of want."[7] Human beings are not beasts. We come first in dignity over the rest of creation. Kuyper's point, rather, is that we should not confuse "first in dignity" with "alone in dignity."

This insight represents the broader point from chapter 1 that freedom entails responsibility. Just because people can own animals doesn't mean that they have a "right" to let them starve to death, for example. Rather, their right over them as property entails a responsibility to care for them, even if the eventual goal is to fatten them, slaughter them, and then use their meat to feed other people or themselves. In the first case (starvation), no human need is being met, and the animals' natures as living beings are not being respected. In the second case, the animals' needs are met up to the point that the animal is used to meet human needs. In doing so, we acknowledge God's purpose for the things he made and ultimately owns.

Property is a broad concept. Economists distinguish between different types of property: land and capital. Land in Economish is a broad term, meaning basically natural resources like soil, minerals, water, air, plants, and animals. Capital refers to any human-made resources meant to be used for other human-made products like tools, machines, and buildings. Lastly, we can also add consumer goods, things made by people for people to use for their own needs, like hamburgers, basketballs, or iPhones. We'll explore that more a little later.

One of the most obvious facts about land is that it is scarce, which is just Economish for "finite" or "limited." Scarcity does not, however, mean that resources are static. We live in a growing, developing, temporal world. Some resources, such as paper, are renewable. Renewable does not just mean "replaceable" either. Renewable resources can be multiplied. One tree can produce hundreds of seeds, which can all grow into new trees themselves.

Other resources, such as metals, are reusable. If your car breaks down and is too expensive to fix, you can still sell it to the salvage yard for scrap metal.

This is an important point because people sometimes approach economic problems as if the number of resources we have and the products we can make from them is fixed. The problem, if that were the case, would be one of *division*. In reality, we can and do *multiply*. For example, what do you do if you have a birthday party and, unexpectedly, too many people come? Do you divide the cake into tiny little pieces? Well, that's one solution, but nobody ends up with much in that scenario. Alternatively, you could bake or buy a second cake.

For most of human history, people were pretty stuck in fixed-pie, single cake, division mentality with regard to wealth. Some economists refer to this as the "zero-sum" fallacy; the mistaken assumption that if one person has more, other people must necessarily have less. In the last two hundred years human beings have really improved when it comes to multiplication. Wealth, though finite, is not fixed. It can be, and is, created. For example, take a look at figure 1.[8]

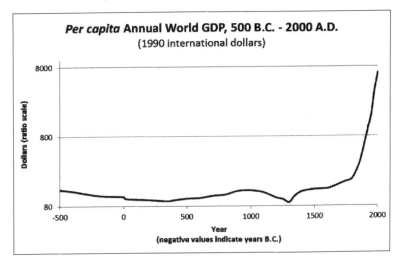

Figure 1

This graph is sometimes referred to as the "hockey stick" of economic history because it resembles a hockey stick lying on its shaft with the foot pointing upward. The big jump in GDP per capita comes right around 1800 or so, although there is a pretty clear upward trend for a few centuries before that as well (the heel of the stick). The left side of the graph could be stretched to the beginning of human history and the line wouldn't go up or down all that much. Something big has happened. We've learned how to multiply.

According to Jordan Ballor,

> What makes these economic gains even more astounding is that there has been a simultaneous population explosion. There are many more "capita" included in the "per capita" as the chart moves to the right, yet we still see enormous gains in per-capita GDP.[9]

Malthus's theory about population was that while we can increase crops arithmetically, people reproduce geometrically. In English: Crops add but people multiply. Because of this, over the course of a few generations, people will reproduce faster than our capacity to feed them. There can only be enough for everyone to eat if something else checks our population, such as war, disease, or— his preferred option—chastity. Otherwise, our population will be checked by starvation. Thus, even if a society could avoid war and disease, people would still do themselves in through reproduction. The commands to "be fruitful" and "multiply" were in conflict. So ... yeah, it was a pretty gloomy picture. In his defense, Malthus wrote about this in 1798, when the big jump was just starting. His analysis is pretty accurate for all of human history before his time. Economists even sometimes refer to this period or state as the "Malthusian trap."

But why does this matter? Well, for one thing, the big upward shift has helped us to become more fruitful and to better care for creation and other human persons, though not without additional challenges, such as social changes, pollution, and materialism. To put things in a more positive perspective, however, I am reminded of St. Paul. After his dramatic conversion experience (see Acts 9), Saints Peter, James, and John sent him to be a missionary. Paul records their charge in his Epistle to the Galatians: "They desired only that we should remember the poor, the very thing which I also was eager to do" (Gal. 2:10).

Of course, a person's heart and soul is most important, but as Vladimir Solovyov put it, "It is written that man does not live by bread *alone*, but it is not written that he lives without bread."[10] Caring for the poor has been a top priority for the church from its beginning, and as President Calvin Coolidge put it, "In all experience, the accumulation of wealth means the multiplication of schools, the increase of knowledge, the dissemination of intelligence, the encouragement of science, the broadening of outlook, the expansion of liberties, the widening of culture."[11] That is, it means better quality of life, even beyond material well-being, for the majority of people, including the poor, and to that extent it is a good thing.

Since 1800, we have, finally, been able to both "be fruitful" and "multiply," without one undermining the other. Instead of the vast majority of people being stuck in crushing poverty, poverty has been on the decline. Really. Even in the last thirty years, extreme poverty across the world has been cut in half. The big differences are industrialization—when technology is combined with increased division of labor—and increased economic freedom, that is, private property rights, freedom of exchange, rule of law, and so on. This leads societies to shift away from agrarian economies stuck in the Mathusian trap.

The economist Joseph Schumpeter called this phenomenon "creative destruction." The idea is simple. The innovation of new markets, techniques, and products displaces old ones, resulting in monumental economic gains. Think of how the assembly line and the automobile put most blacksmiths out of business. We should not minimize the harm done to blacksmiths, but we should also not overlook the great gains for the vast majority of people—not just the factory workers but everyone who benefited from cars and trucks through shipping, increased mobility, and so on. "[T]he contents of the laborer's budget, say from 1760 to 1940, did not simply grow on unchanging lines but they underwent a process of qualitative change," wrote Schumpeter in 1942. And for the most part, on a global scale it has continued to increase since then. The increase was not just more of the same life but a better life altogether. It was accomplished through "a history of revolutions," highlighting the central role of the entrepreneur for economic development. This, he claimed, is "the essential fact about capitalism."[12] It is what caused and what drives the hockey stick phenomenon of sustained economic growth that more and more people benefit from every day.

In addition, as the economist Deirdre McCloskey has pointed out,[13] at the same time there had been a growing shift in people's perspectives toward merchants, bankers, and other trades as well as private property and commerce in general. These professions and the institutions that make them possible were often looked down on as unproductive and exploitive because, so it was thought, they make money off of the goods of others. Isn't that just greed?

As it turns out, however, most people can't start a business without a loan, and most businesses need shops to sell their merchandise for them and transportation companies to ship it all over the world. It is not as if these things didn't exist before 1800, but the negative stigma that accompanied these professions at times led to strong regulations, sanctions, and cultural mores against them. A mother wouldn't have been happy if her son became a banker, for example. McCloskey believes that it was a shift in people's attitudes regarding the dignity of these professions that made the difference.

I'm not sure which factor is the chicken and which are the eggs. It seems that innovation, property, trade, dignity, and the division of labor all played a role. Of these, we still need to take a look at work. All the capital in the world won't produce civilization without human labor. People and their labor are at the center of all economies just as much as the resources of the earth and the capital produced from them. But what is work?

Through Human Labor

"Work," wrote the Reformed theologian Lester DeKoster, "is the form in which we make ourselves useful to others."[14] I like this definition because it puts things in a realistic, everyday perspective. Certainly, people can work just because they want a paycheck to spend on themselves alone. That might be greedy, but we need to be careful not to confuse profit with greed. People work in order to profit, but profit is not good or evil in itself. That judgment depends on the circumstances in which it was gained and the use to which it is put. And as DeKoster points out, our work itself is service to others. If it wasn't, they wouldn't pay us to do it in the first place, and most people wouldn't want to do it for free. It's an exchange.

The division of labor is the phenomenon that the more the manufacturing of individual components of an eventual, finished product can be broken down into separate jobs, the more efficiently it can be produced. Adam Smith offered the classic example of the pin-maker:

> One man draws out the wire, another straightens it, a third cuts it, a fourth points it, a fifth grinds it at the top for receiving the head; to make the head requires two or three distinct operations; to put it on, is a peculiar business, to whiten the pins is another; it is even a trade by itself to put them into the paper; and the important business of making a pin is, in this manner, divided into about eighteen distinct operations, which, in some manufactories, are all performed by distinct hands, though in others the same man will sometimes perform two or three of them.[15]

While he doubts that someone uneducated in pin-making could make more than even one pin a day, and even an experienced worker could make up to twenty at the most, Smith observes that ten persons who have divided the labor in this way produced "about twelve pounds of pins in a day." How many is that? "There are in a pound upwards of four thousand pins of a middling size. Those ten persons, therefore, could make among them upwards of forty-eight thousand pins in a day."[16]

Another way to think of it is the power of human cooperation. We might say that the division of labor, then, is just Economish for "teamwork." When people work together (literally), they are able to multiply the fruits of their labors far beyond what they could each do alone. As we saw in chapter 2, God made us to flourish in communion with each other. Ten people working alone might be able to produce ten pins total in a single day, maybe up to two hundred (twenty each) if they were really good, but nowhere near forty-eight thousand.

It is worth noting as well that this mass production did not in any way change the quality of the pins produced. Sometimes that is the case with products today, but it is not necessarily true. In this case, it was simply by splitting up the labor required to make a pin into each of its parts and then assigning a single task to each person that made all the difference. Because they could make so many so much faster, they could lower the price to consumers while still making astronomically higher profits. It's a win-win.

Our world is full of examples of this. Consider this book. If you are reading the print version, the paper came from trees that were felled by bearded lumberjacks wearing red flannel and suspenders (or so I imagine), made into paper in factories, then shipped to a printer. Similarly, the ink for the words and the cover had to be manufactured too. And all of the factories involved used tools that had to be made somewhere else, by someone else, at some time before. All of the vehicles used to transport the capital that would become this book had to be made by people all over the world, working to provide for their families and, unknowingly, to provide this book for you. If you're using an e-reader, well, there are far more people and resources involved. Nearly every product, every fruit of the cultivation of creation, connects us with nearly every other human being on the planet. And their collective contributions make this book more affordable while also benefiting more people in the process. (Thanks, guys!) In this way, our work connects us with other people, serves their needs through products and property, provides for us, and fulfills one of the purposes for which God made us.

For the Provision of Human Needs

I suppose I don't really *need* a Starbucks decaf peppermint mocha, but I'm happy that I can enjoy one every now and then. (Let's pause here and wait for a few readers to walk across the room and pick the book back up again.) The people who work at Starbucks, however, *do* need an income, and my purchase helps provide that for them, at least that's what I tell myself. (Victor Claar isn't listening, is he?)

Without demand for their products, businesses go bankrupt and all the people that work for them lose their jobs and incomes. "Demand" is Economish for the combination of desire and means.

That is, I can cry out to the heavens for a flying car, but that desire is not economically significant unless someone else is able to create one and sell it at a price I can afford. Thus, the means to get a product need to be there for my desire to be considered demand.

We demand things for all sorts of motivations. Economists aren't too interested in what those motivations may be. They tend to collapse them all into the term "self-interest," which doesn't necessarily mean selfishness, though many people (including many economists) do take it that way. Rather, self-interest is really just Economish for "self-*determined* interest." It's basically an empty set that can be anything—whether greed, altruism, fear, jealousy, love, or something else—that may motivate a person to demand a particular consumer good. Of course, these motivations certainly matter from a moral point of view, underscoring the fact that economics is not all of life. But economists, as economists, see "the outward appearance," while "the LORD looks at the heart" (1 Sam. 16:7). In their defense, so does everyone else. Even if through surveys social scientists might be able to get a general idea about the motivations of others, at the end of the day, we really only know our own heart for sure—if even that. If we are concerned about our own motivations, we need to put in the work of daily asceticism to begin to change them.

As I've already said, consumer goods, unlike capital, are things people make that are not used to make other things. The line between consumer goods and capital can be a little fuzzy though. For example, if I buy a wrench for my home maintenance needs, that wrench is a consumer good because it is just being used for my needs around the home. However, if my son Brendan becomes a mechanic when he grows up, and I give him that same wrench as a gift to use in his work, then it is capital.

So when economists talk about consumption, they basically mean "using stuff for your own needs." It does not necessarily imply destroying or wasting or eating things. I don't recommend trying to eat a wrench at least. The point is that if you buy one to help you build your kid's new swing set, you're consuming that wrench as far as economists are concerned. Consumption is usually measured by household, and it is a better indicator than income when it comes to measuring people's quality of life. While no metric is perfect, consumption figures tell us how much and what people actually use in a given context, thus factoring in cost of living, social service transfer benefits, and support from others within or beyond the household. Income measures don't include those things, making them less useful for comparison. The cost of rent in Grand Rapids, Michigan, is a lot less than New York City, for example. But both can be counted as consumption of shelter of a specific size, indicating that even though incomes may be higher in New York City, quality of life may come out about the same (or less or more) when we look at what those incomes actually allow a person to consume.

All this talk about consumption raises an important question, however. At what point does consumption become *consumerism*? Consumerism has become a buzzword. No doubt, it can be a problem. But to define it as "wanting to consume stuff" is sorely inadequate and may even require assuming that consumption is inherently sinful. Orthodox priest Fr. Gregory Jensen explains why this is a problem:

> If consumption is immoral, if the goal of our economic life is to consume less, then we ought to dismiss the economic gains of the last two centuries as also being immoral. Assuming this, however, reflects not only a lack of gratitude to God for his material blessings but it also condemns our neighbor to poverty.[17]

He continues,

> As in all other areas of my life, in my economic decisions I need to be on guard against my own sinfulness. This means that I should not imagine that *my abstention* is necessarily any morally better than *your consumption*; both are tainted by sin, even as both can be a source of goodness for self and others.[18]

As we've already seen, to quote the Orthodox theologian Fr. Alexander Schmemann, "In the biblical story of creation man is presented, first of all, as a hungry being, and the whole world as his food."[19] Jesus expects us to ask God for "our daily bread" (Matt. 6:11). And traditionally, at the center of Christian worship is the bread and wine of the Eucharist, which the Roman

Catholic mass rightly notes are the "fruit of the earth and work of human hands."[20] They're consumer goods!

So consumption is not inherently sinful but a natural part of human life and even essential to the supernatural life of the sacraments. As Jensen put it, "If consumption were not a good thing, then the reception of Holy Communion would be a sin."[21] Saint John Chrysostom offers a helpful way to put this in perspective: "neither is wealth an evil, but the having made a bad use of wealth; nor is poverty a virtue, but the having made a virtuous use of poverty."[22] Virtue and vice are good and evil, respectively. Wealth is only good or evil to the extent that it is done virtuously or viciously. That does not mean, however, that wealth does not bring greater occasion for temptation, or poverty greater opportunity for virtue. But it does mean that wealth and poverty do not of themselves make a person evil or good. As Chrysostom explains, referencing Jesus's parable of the rich man and Lazarus (Luke 16:19–31),

> That rich man who was in the time of Lazarus was punished, not because he was rich, but because he was cruel and inhuman. And that poor man who rested in the bosom of Abraham was praised, not because he was poor, but because he had borne his poverty with thankfulness.[23]

We ought to be more watchful of our souls than our wealth, whether we are rich or poor.

Jensen offers a better definition of consumerism:

> Consumerism is really nothing more or less than human consumption unredeemed by Christ. Consumerism is consumption that conforms to the standards of this world rather than those of Christ. Consumerism is consumption that has not yet been "transformed" ascetically and has not yet been made "good and acceptable" according to the "perfect will of God" (Rom. 12:2).[24]

But how do we do that? How do we make sure that we are using the fruits of our labors in the way that God intended them? We've already said the answer: virtue. And we've already said how to get it: asceticism, or spiritual discipline.

More specifically, some people can afford to be pickier with their consumption. Think again of fair trade coffee. Victor Claar says it isn't really fair, but there are all sorts of similar ways that people monitor their own consumption, from *Consumer Reports* to Amazon ratings to labels indicating ingredients, ethical standards, or eco-friendliness. Any number of these may be just as flawed as the fair trade label for coffee, but that is a matter for personal research. Some may be reliable and accurate. And the variety and proliferation of these labels demonstrates that there is significant demand for products that at least appear to follow a higher standard.

Nevertheless, they are a luxury many people simply do not have. Either they can't afford the greater price of "better" products, or they lack the time or expertise to evaluate such ratings. Anybody, however, can practice a little self-reflection and awareness. This can be as simple as stopping to say grace before a meal or remembering to thank the clerk at the local department store. Asceticism is not so much about consuming less as it is about learning to consume differently, putting our various needs and wants in their rightful places.

For example, for those of us who practice it, fasting from meat during Lent is meant to cultivate gratitude for the meat—and everything else—that we enjoy at other times of the year, as well as for God's provision for our needs, through human economic activity, all throughout the year. Confusing our spiritual practice with the goal of our spiritual lives is just as much of an error as is consumerism. I would even say that such false asceticism is but another kind of consumerism. To believe that just because one eats vegetables instead of meat one is therefore more righteous or holy or in any other way "better" than someone else, is also to consume according to "the standards of this world" and derive one's value from that consumption. Rather, as St. Paul put it, "Let not him who eats despise him who does not eat, and let not him who does not eat judge him who eats; for God has received him. Who are you to judge another's servant?" (Rom. 14:3–4).

Through Relationships of Exchange

When a supply and a demand really love one another, they come together and an exchange is born. Networks of exchange are called markets. And economies are made of countless interconnected markets. If there is no market for a product, it means that demand does not meet supply—no one wants what is being sold at that price and thus there is no exchange, no market for that product in that economy.

Studying markets can be enlightening. Too often, economic questions are reduced to ideologies and partisanships. Either something is capitalist and good or socialist and bad, or pro-business or pro-consumer, and so on. While I do think these words can have meaning and use, I don't think people often enough have sufficiently precise definitions in mind. Moreover, even knowing those definitions often does little to help understand any *particular* market, not to mention whole economies.

To help clarify, I commend the work of the German economist Walter Eucken. With Wilhelm Röpke and Ludwig Erhard (all devout Christians, incidentally), Eucken significantly contributed to West Germany's post-World War II economic miracle. A country torn apart economically by central planning, literally by bombs, and spiritually by an inhuman ideology became one of the strongest economies in Europe only a decade later, and it remains so to the present day. That recovery is about the best recommendation any economist could hope for: Their policies were tried, and they worked! So what can Eucken teach us about markets?

In his *Foundations of Economics,* Eucken provides a chart (simplified in figure 2) by which a person can analyze any market in any economy at any time ever.[25]

Form of Supply / Form of Demand	Competition	Oligopoly	Monopoly
Competition	Perfect Competition	Supply Oligopoly	Supply Monopoly
Oligopoly	Demand Oligopoly	Bilateral Oligopoly	Limited Supply Monopoly
Monopoly	Demand Monopoly	Limited Demand Monopoly	Bilateral Monopoly

Figure 2

There's a lot of Economish to translate here, so be patient (it is, after all, a virtue). We've already covered supply and demand. First, then, we need to talk about competition. Economist and rabbi Israel Kirzner has pointed out, "To the layman, the term *competition* undoubtedly conveys the notion of men vigorously *competing* with others, each striving to deliver a performance that outdistances his rivals." Of course. What else would it mean? Well, he goes on to say that "the term *competition* in economic theory is used in just the *opposite* sense."[26] Basically, to use a crude example, it's like how the word *pissed* means totally different things to an American or an Englishman. To the first, it means "angry." To the second, it means "drunk." I suppose a person can be pissed in both ways at the same time, but the meanings are still quite different. Competition is one of those words, except replace "American" with "economist" and "Englishman" with "normal person."

Kirzner is really helpful in that his own theory seeks to take the commonsense definition of competition seriously, and we'll return to him in a moment. First, however, we need to explain the Economish version. Basically, a perfectly competitive market is one in which the presence of other market actors produces equilibrium, that happy middle point where supply and demand meet with the least amount of waste. If a supplier—say, Nintendo—only has one or a few people in cahoots that demand its product (a demand monopoly or oligopoly, respectively), then that person or group can talk them down further than they would like. They need to recover as much as possible of the costs of producing whatever video game, gadget, or card game they've created. But with few buyers they are forced to take what they can get.

Notice that economic value, which is measured through the price system, is determined by the subjective (i.e., personal) preferences of potential consumers. If most potential buyers aren't interested, prices plummet. Conversely, the higher the demand, the greater the price can be. Economic value, then, is an entirely different kind of value than moral value or artistic value or any other sort of value. Being its own distinct sphere of life, economics has its own internal logic. This doesn't mean that economic value is all that matters but simply that it is real and important.

Economic value, interestingly, is increased through exchange. Prices measure the subjective preference of all the demanders in a market relative to the costs and output of the suppliers. If I want a candy bar more than my dollar, and the candy store owner wants my dollar more than his candy bar, we both gain something through exchange. Total economic value in society increases. Free prices miraculously coordinate millions of little bits of vital, subjective information essential to any well-functioning economy, as Friedrich Hayek pointed out.[27] Only God is omniscient, and only God knows our hearts. Without that total knowledge, the price system seems to be the best means we have for coordinating all that important information.

Now let's look at the supply side. Nintendo is the only video game company that makes Mario games. They alone own the trademark and rights to that beloved Japanese stereotype of an Italian plumber and all his friends and enemies (which, I guess, are mostly reptiles?). Thus, Nintendo has a supply monopoly on Mario. If there were high demand and no comparable alternative games, Nintendo could charge far more than the standard video game price for its Mario games. Prices go up when the demand for the few available products is higher. Given that Nintendo does have this monopoly, why doesn't this happen? Why aren't they able to charge higher prices for their Mario games?

The answer is the Economish term "substitute goods." If a competitor makes a comparable game to Mario, which we'll call Blario, then most people won't save extra to buy the high-priced Mario game when they can get Super Blario Brothers for the standard price. *Some* people will, and sometimes settling into the reality that one's product is a luxury item is completely viable. That, however, is rare for video games. Similarly, some potential buyers will simply purchase or continue to play previous Mario games rather than the newest one, waiting for the price to come down to the point where they'd actually pay for it. In this case, older versions of the same product act as substitute goods.

Think of how some people are actually content with an older model Android or iPhone, even when a new shiny model has just been released. Some people might even purchase the used phones of friends or family members who just bought the new one. For them, the old phones are substitute goods that keep them from demanding the newer model. In these ways, competition pushes markets toward equilibrium prices. Kirzner's complaint is that if at equilibrium everyone is happy, who's really competing anymore? Again, I'll get to that in a minute, but we're not done with Eucken's chart.

So Eucken gives us all the various markets we can possibly encounter. For those of us who value low prices and low waste, perfect competition is the best. But not all markets are competitive, and in some cases they might not be able to be competitive anytime soon. What then? In order to illustrate this, consider the often controversial example of labor unions. Let's say that in one town, a big car manufacturer is nearly the sole demander of labor. Of course, people work at grocery stores and gas stations and whatnot too, but the factory has a partial demand monopoly (the bottom row of Eucken's chart). If it wasn't there, the town's whole economy would go bust. The workers are the suppliers here, and there are so many of them with only one place to work that supply can be considered competitive (the left column of Eucken's chart). What if they don't like their wages or benefits or hours? The company has little reason to adjust its contracts. They could, of course, move to another town where there are more options for employment. But that's costly, and there are a lot of important, noneconomic reasons why someone may not want to leave their hometown. Economics is not all of life. People have family, friends, and other group ties such as a home church. The cost of leaving cannot really be measured by a price. They do have another option though: organization.

When workers in the town form a union, they collectively bargain for contracts with the big auto factory. Kuyper would point out that as labor is its own distinct sphere, and because our societies are not mere aggregates of atomistic individuals, they should certainly be free to do so.[28] Pope Pius XI even criticized those in his time and before who supported "denying the natural right to form associations to those who needed it most to defend themselves from ill treatment at the hands of the powerful."[29] By putting their lots together in solidarity, workers form a supply oligopoly (the middle row of Eucken's chart).[30] This creates a limited-demand monopoly market for manufacturing labor (the bottom-middle square). The company may have some monopoly power, but it still needs labor, and together workers have more power to negotiate than alone.

Typically, this labor supply oligopoly is also partial in that employers will often use temporary workers for new projects, whose wages are comparatively low, benefits nonexistent, and who must hope that they can stay on and join the union to improve their situation. So one can work at the factory without being in the union, but the union sets the standard, and temporary employment falls far short. In many cases, though not all, the union will also manage to close the labor supply to competitors: that is, one union per shop and all nontemporary workers must join the union. This creates a significant barrier to entry for any workers who would want to enter that market, and it also creates extra barriers to promotion beyond being based on merit alone.

Additionally, because big companies and unions often have extra power and resources, they are able to lobby for legislation that further protects their market position at the expense of new-comers. This is commonly called "cronyism" or "crony capitalism," because the market actors secure their position not by offering better products (wages and benefits from employers; quality of labor from employees) but rather by knowing the right legislators and brokering deals that regulate markets in their favor by closing them to potential competitors. As a result, these legislators might even tout their records for being pro-business or pro-labor. This is called "cronyism" because the interest groups succeed not through merit in the market but through their *relationships* to lawmakers. It is a distortion of the sphere of government, which shouldn't play favorites. When it comes to economics and law, the more impersonal they can be the better, because *impersonal* in this case is simply another word for impartial. Without impartiality, there can be no rule of law, no equality before the law, and no justice.

This brings me to another of Eucken's important distinctions, and it brings me back to Kirzner. Eucken notes that supply and demand can be either closed or open. Unions have some benefits in checking the power of employers in a monopoly situation, but typically it comes at the cost of making markets more closed. They need not do so, but that is often the case. A market with open labor supply, by contrast, would be one where workers at the same factory could form a competing union or simply negotiate contracts on an individual basis, being free to work without joining any union if they wished. Getting this distinction between open and closed markets is really important, because this, above anything else, is what determines whether or not a market is free and what opens the possibility that any given market may move toward the ideal of perfect competition.

For Kirzner, competition is not a static state of equilibrium but a dynamic force that drives the process of markets evolving toward the ideal state that can never be fully achieved because it would require perfect knowledge of all possible opportunities. Instead, Kirzner's competition can only exist when there is disequilibrium. And there always is, to some degree. There is always an opportunity to profit by closing formerly unseen gaps between supply and demand that create waste. In this sense, Kirzner is using the commonsense (normal person) definition of competition: It is the attempt to outdo one's competitors, to do better than the current standard. He uses the term *pure entre-*

preneur to describe the person who sees some people buying at a higher price than necessary and other people selling for too low. The pure entrepreneur need not be a business owner at all, just someone who sees and acts on this opportunity. Through that intuition, this entrepreneur bridges the gap of imperfect information, buying for a little more from the sellers and selling for a little less to the buyers. As a result, the buyers and sellers get a deal and the entrepreneur profits. It's a win-win-win that eliminates waste in a market and, by extension, in economies.

So how do we maximize this important driving force of economic advancement? Kirzner says that

> there can be no doubt that the necessary and sufficient condition for competition to exist without obstacle is complete freedom of entry into all kinds of market activity. When we assert that purely entrepreneurial activity is *always* competitive, we are then asserting that *with respect to purely entrepreneurial activity no possible obstacles to freedom of entry can exist.*[31]

This is what *free markets* ought to mean. Free markets are open markets. They are not whatever a self-declared capitalist or pro-business pundit or politician says, but the minimization of barriers to entry to markets for all people, creating the maximum opportunity for the entrepreneurial innovations that raise wages, increase employment, lower costs and prices, and that have driven the great and amazing hockey stick of economic history from the beginning of the Industrial Revolution to today. In other words, it should be about the economic conditions, and their moral foundation, wherein people are best able to freely cultivate creation for the provision of human needs, for the good of their neighbors and themselves, and for the glory of God.

Discussion Questions

1. What are your responsibilities to your property?
2. How do you serve others with your work?
3. In what ways can you be less judgmental and more grateful about the things you consume?
4. How many different markets do you participate in every day? What are they? How would they be classified according to Walter Eucken's chart? How does that classification affect you?
5. How do you understand the term *free markets*? How does the author's definition challenge yours? How might his definition be improved?

Notes

1. Hugh of St. Victor, *Didascalicon*, trans. Jerome Taylor (New York; London: Columbia University Press, 1961), 2.23, 77.

2. Thomas Carlyle, "Occasional Discourse on the Negro Question," *Fraser's Magazine for Town and Country* 40 (December 1849): 677. This essay was originally published anonymously.

3. Carlyle, "Occasional Discourse," 676–77.

4. Carlyle, "Occasional Discourse," 670.

5. Abraham Kuyper, "Commentary on the Heidelberg Catechism Lord's Day 42 (1895)," trans. Albert Gootjes, *Journal of Markets & Morality* 16, no. 2 (Fall 2013): 723. Henceforth: "Lord's Day 42."

6. Kuyper, "Lord's Day 42," 730.

7. Kuyper, "Lord's Day 42," 730.

8. Source: Victor V. Claar, "The Urgency of Poverty and the Hope of Genuinely Fair Trade," *Journal of Markets & Morality* 16, no. 1 (Spring 2013): 274.

9. Jordan J. Ballor, "Life to the Full: The Dangers of Material Wealth and Spiritual Poverty," *Public Discourse*, September 25, 2014.

10. Vladimir Solovyov, *The Justification of the Good*, trans. Natalie Dudington, ed. Boris Jakim (Grand Rapids: Eerdmans, 2005), 394–95.

11. Calvin Coolidge, "The Press under a Free Government," Address before the American Society of Newspaper Editors, Washington, DC, January 17, 1925, available at *Calvin Coolidge Presidential Foundation*, https://coolidgefoundation.org/resources/speeches-as-president-1923-1929-16/.

12. Joseph Schumpeter, *Capitalism, Socialism, Democracy*, 3rd ed. (New York: Harper & Row, 1950), 83.

13. See Deirdre McCloskey, *Bourgeois Dignity: Why Economics Can't Explain the Modern World* (Chicago: University of Chicago Press, 2011).

14. Lester DeKoster, *Work: The Meaning of Your Life—A Christian Perspective* (1982; repr., Grand Rapids: Christian's Library Press, 2015), 1.

15. Adam Smith, *An Inquiry into the Nature and Causes of the Wealth of Nations*, vol. 1, Glasgow Edition of the Works of Adam Smith, vol. 2 (1976; repr., Indianapolis: LibertyClassics, 1981), 15. Henceforth: *Wealth of Nations*.

16. Smith, *Wealth of Nations*, 1:15.

17. Gregory Jensen, *The Cure For Consumerism* (Grand Rapids: Acton Institute, 2015), 90.

18. Jensen, *The Cure for Consumerism*, 93.

19. Alexander Schmemann, *For the Life of the World: Sacraments and Orthodoxy* (1963; repr., Crestwood, NY: St Vladimir's Seminary Press, 1988), 11.

20. United States Conference of Catholic Bishops, *The Roman Missal* (Chicago: Liturgy Training Publications, 2011), 749.

21. Jensen, *The Cure for Consumerism*, 142n6.

22. John Chrysostom, *Homily against Publishing the Errors of the Brethren* in *NPNF*[1] 9:236.

23. Chrysostom, *Homily against Publishing the Errors*, 236.

24. Jensen, *The Cure For Consumerism*, 145.

25. Adapted from Walter Eucken, *The Foundations of Economics: History and Theory in the Analysis of Economic Reality*, trans. T. W. Hutchinson (Chicago: University of Chicago Press, 1951), 158.

26. Israel M. Kirzner, *Competition and Entrepreneurship* (Chicago: University of Chicago Press, 1979), 89.

27. See Friedrich A. Hayek, "The Use of Knowledge in Society," *American Economic Review* 35, no. 4 (September 1945): 519–30.

28. See Abraham Kuyper, "Manual Labor (1889)," in *Abraham Kuyper: A Centennial Reader*, ed. James D. Bratt (Grand Rapids: Eerdmans, 1998), 231–54.

29. Pope Pius XI, Encyclical Letter *Quadragesimo Anno*, May 15, 1931, http://w2.vatican.va/content/pius-xi/en/encyclicals/documents/hf_p-xi_enc_19310515_quadragesimo-anno.html, 30.

30. It could also be considered a monopoly if the union itself is considered the sole supplier of labor rather than a group of suppliers (the workers) in cahoots. The effects described herein are the same. These categories should not be taken more strictly than the actual reality allows.

31. Kirzner, *Competition and Entrepreneurship*, 99.

Part 2

WHAT IF?

4

Property and Prices

We have been turned out of Paradise. We have neither eternal life nor unlimited means of gratification. Everywhere we turn, if we choose one thing, we must relinquish others which, in different circumstances, we would wish not to have relinquished. Scarcity of means to satisfy given ends is an almost ubiquitous condition of human behaviour.

—Lionel Robbins[1]

Introduction

Back in 1995, when I was eleven, I was a fan of the science fiction show *Sliders*. Looking back, the show doesn't hold up—the special effects are sometimes laughable and the writing and acting now seem corny. But for eleven-year-old me, the show imaginatively explored all sorts of fun ideas. It was great.

The basic premise of the show: Genius grad student Quinn Mallory (played by Jerry O'Connell) opens a portal to alternate worlds where he and three friends get trapped, unable to find their way back home, "sliding" from world to world each episode. This show didn't feature space travel, though. Rather it was the "same planet, different dimension," as Mallory explained in the opening title sequence.

Every episode had the same basic formula. The sliders would land in a different world that explored various What if? questions. What if the colonists had lost the American Revolutionary War? What if we had never discovered penicillin? What if men were considered the "weaker sex" and women historically dominated positions of power, including the United States president (who, that episode postulated, was none other than Hillary Clinton!)? You get the idea.

In a sense, part 2 of this book is like a season of *Sliders*. Each section of this chapter and the next is like an episode that features a world in which one or more basic economic concepts are ignored, as if they had never been discovered. Unfortunately, unlike *Sliders*, this isn't science fiction. It's the same planet, same dimension. For many people in the world (and for everyone in varying degrees), this is reality, and that reality is more often tragic than entertaining. To be clear, while there are various schools of economic thought, and I have my own preferences among them, the concepts explored here are truly basic. A left-leaning economist like Nobel Laureate and *New York Times* columnist Paul Krugman is just as likely to acknowledge the benefits of private property or international trade, for example, as a free-market economist like George Mason University's Tyler Cowen. For the most part, both the left-leaning Progressive Policy Institute and the libertarian Cato Institute would be in agreement on these issues as well. The disagreements between schools of thought tend to be much more subtle than I can explore here.

This is not to say that this whole section is purely economic. That would run against the entire purpose of this book. Life is economic, but economics is not all of life. So while other more capable writers have written books and essays that undertake this sort of thought experiment, my version will still be unique in its specifically theological orientation.

In the previous chapters, we began with Genesis. Having discussed the three relationships outlined there—humans and God, humans and other people, humans and the world—these chapters seek to further integrate them by looking at what happens when people fail to be prudent and instead ignore the God-given structures of social life. As it turns out, Genesis has something to say about that too.

We've talked about how sin, corruption, and death have complicated our development as the people God made us to be, but we never looked at the actual story Genesis tells of how this happened. This is not the sort of book that can answer debates about the extent to which such stories are meant to be taken historically or symbolically. Rather, I will conveniently sidestep that discussion and instead bring to the Scripture a simple question that transcends it: What happens when we ignore God's plan for us and the world?

In the first two chapters of Genesis, God makes the world and everything in it. Then he makes the first man and woman, and he places them in a beautiful garden in Eden and gives them a few instructions: be fruitful and multiply, till the ground, exercise dominion, and one last one: "Of every tree of the garden you may freely eat; but of the tree of the knowledge of good and evil you shall not eat, for in the day that you eat of it you shall surely die" (Gen. 2:16–17).

Now, there was nothing inherently bad about this tree. In fact, since God made it, surely it was good. But God makes things "according to their kinds," with their own natures and purposes as part of a harmonious whole, a cosmos. There is a right way to interact with the world (and with ourselves and each other) that honors those natures and fulfills those purposes. But there are wrong ways too. This is the essence of natural law. In this case, God told the man and the woman that the fruit of this tree was off limits. They would have to fast from it, or they would "surely die." Why that may be, I have no idea; God did not elaborate. Intelligent theologians have speculated about the precise nature of this tree for ages. I've found no conclusive answer, but most everyone agrees on what happened afterward.

Genesis 3 tells the story of how, tempted by a serpent, the woman and the man who was right there "with her" (Gen. 3:6) took and ate from the tree. Why?

> When the woman saw that the tree was good for food, that it was pleasant to the eyes, and a tree desirable to make one wise, she took of its fruit and ate. She also gave to her husband with her, and he ate. Then the eyes of both of them were opened, and they knew that they were naked; and they sewed fig leaves together and made themselves coverings. (Gen. 3:6–7)

What was the problem here? God made the tree. So it likely really was "good for food" and "pleasant to the eyes." And it's called "the tree of the knowledge of good and evil," so it probably even was "desirable to make one wise." It is not what "the woman saw" that was the problem, but what she and her husband didn't see.

The serpent had said, "You will not surely die. For God knows that in the day you eat of it your eyes will be opened, and you will be like God, knowing good and evil" (Gen. 3:4–5). And "the eyes of both of them were opened." But what did that knowledge bring?—"they knew that they were naked." Little children don't know this. Trust me, I'm a father. They may know that they aren't wearing any clothes, but that doesn't stop them from climbing out of the bathtub and dancing around the living room. Rather, to know oneself as naked in the sense described here is to know oneself as exposing to others what should be concealed. It is not simply to be unclothed, but to be *ashamed* of it. This contrasts sharply with how things were: "And they were both naked, the man and his wife, and were not ashamed" (Gen. 2:25).

Saint James explores the psychology of this: "when desire has conceived, it gives birth to sin; and sin, when it is full-grown, brings forth death" (James 1:15). Having given in to desire and disregarded God's plan for the tree, a whole host of desires, and with them fears, poured out of their hearts. Seeing themselves with newly opened eyes, eyes now aware not only of what is good but also of what is evil, they fear being open with one another or even themselves. They are naked and ashamed. They now have need for modesty, which though a cardinal virtue is one that comes only from a greater sense of temptation, danger, and obligation. Innocence has no knowledge of modesty.

This same story plays out in all of our lives. As children, we are not ashamed; in that sense we are innocent. But as we mature and grow in knowledge, we also find ourselves more tempted, realize the corruption of our desires, and become more ashamed with every sin as we see the destruction—the death—that comes with it. Out of fear of that death, we multiply our desires for fleeting comforts, hence multiplying the source of our fears and on and on until we die in the more conventional sense. This is why, for Christians, the resurrection of Jesus Christ is so nec- essary for our salvation. It gives us victory over death, transfiguring even our failures into opportunities for daily resurrection through the ascetic discipline of repentance.

From the perspective of natural law, this phenomenon is always true. Even if we "get away with it," the result of sin is still death. As the church father St. Ambrose of Milan put it, "The wicked man is a punishment to himself, but the upright man is a grace to himself—and to either, whether good or bad, the reward of his deeds is paid in his own person."[2] He explains what he means by this: "The life of the criminal is as a dream." When he wakes from that dream, "He has opened his eyes. His repose has departed, his enjoyment has fled." He continues, "Thou seest the enjoyments of the sinner; but question his conscience. Will he not be more foul than any sepulchre?"[3] God made us for virtue, and we cannot be happy without it, no matter how good our lives may appear. We may look around and think we've got it made, but when our eyes are opened to what really matters, our vision changes and we are left ashamed.

To bring us back to economics, the nineteenth-century French politician Frédéric Bastiat similarly distinguishes between the good and the bad economist with regard to what each sees and doesn't see:

> In the economy, an act, a habit, an institution, a law, gives birth not only to an effect, but to a series of effects. Of these effects, the first only is immediate; it manifests itself simultaneously with its cause—it is seen. The others unfold in succession—they are not seen: it is well for us if they are foreseen. Between a good and a bad economist this constitutes the whole difference—the one takes account of the visible effect; the other takes account both of the effects which are seen and also of those which it is necessary to foresee.[4]

This, too, was the mistake of the man and the woman in the garden. God, being a good economist, foresaw the long term effect of eating from the tree: death. But they saw only the immediate consequence and ignored his warning: "When the woman saw that the tree was good for food, that it was pleasant to the eyes, and a tree desirable to make one wise, she took of its fruit and ate."

Knowing our propensity as human beings to make this error, one of the highest contributions of economic science is to help us avoid it. Now, economics is not all of life, and economists who are good at seeing some things may be blind to others. Nevertheless, we need their insights and the foresight of the economic way of thinking if we want to live with one another in the world God made according to the structure and purpose he gave it. When we don't, as we will see, the consequences are costly. They are built in to the nature of our social life.

Accordingly, in *Sliders*-fashion, part 2 of this book will ask and briefly answer the following questions, with a view to the often-overlooked effects:

1. What if we didn't have *private property*?
2. What if we didn't have *profits*?
3. What if we didn't have *free prices*?
4. What if we didn't have *money*?
5. What if we didn't have *trade*?
6. What if we didn't have *technology*?
7. What if we didn't have *inequality*?
8. What if we didn't have *the rule of law*?
9. What if we didn't have *free markets*?

The answers are not meant to be all-encompassing but only illustrative of how the economic way of thinking can help us to see what often gets overlooked. This chapter examines the first four questions, while chapter 5 will examine the others.

Now, one might object that this "What if?" approach is overly utilitarian or consequentialist, that morally what *really* matters is only our intentions. There is a long tradition of Christians and others insisting on this, dating at least back to the French medieval philosopher Peter Abelard. But as the example of fair trade coffee from the start of this book shows, good intentions can have dire consequences if improperly pursued. The point here is *not* that intentions don't matter. Rather, it is simply that consequences matter *too*, not only economically but also morally. Thus the process is as important as the goal because processes are what determine whether or not we ever actually *achieve* our intentions. Indeed, when some people say that they don't care about the consequences of their actions, I question the goodness of their intentions. *The two cannot be separated.* Thus, when it comes to questions of social justice, we must unite good intentions with sound economics.

Private Property

Every so often, some well-meaning theologian will make the anachronistic claim that the early church was communist, based on Acts 2:44–45: "Now all who believed were together, and had all things in common, and sold their possessions and goods, and divided them among all, as anyone had need." Isn't this the biblical ideal? Isn't property selfish? Wouldn't the world be better without it?[5]

First of all, this is a poor reading of the Scriptures. I already mentioned in the last chapter the implications of the command "you shall not steal," but this passage from Acts presumes private property too. To begin with, what these early Christians did was commendable because it was done as a free response to the grace of salvation. But if there were no property, there would have been nothing to give nor the freedom to give it. Second, the property in question still had an owner: the church, a private organization. They didn't donate their possessions to Caesar but to Christ and his church. If churches and other religious organizations didn't have property rights, they wouldn't enjoy religious freedom either. They would have no power to meet in a designated place in accordance with their traditions and the urging of their consciences. They'd have to get permission from the state and be subject to any regulations that the state deemed necessary. In a place like communist China, where this is currently the case, in some instances these conditions have become oppressive. Expensive new church buildings, funded out of the goodwill of church members, have been bulldozed at the whims of government officials who changed their minds about letting Christians use that land for that purpose.[6]

Third, as Reformed theologians Gerard Berghoef and Lester DeKoster pointed out,

> The early enthusiasm reflected by the initial believers "having all things in common" quickly broke down. The "Hellenists" … murmured that "their widows were neglected in the daily distribution" from the common fund (Acts 6:1), showing that the communal sharing reported earlier (Acts 2:44, and 4:32) lapsed early.

Instead, the solution to this problem was the ordaining of the first deacons. "The office of deacon declares that systematic diakonia [service], rather than forced Communist equality, is the church's inspired answer to disparities in wealth and talent."[7]

Now, it could still be argued that perhaps this, too, is anachronistic. Objections to private property in modern societies respond to concrete societal conditions significantly different from those in the first-century Roman Empire. The nineteenth-century French anarchist Pierre-Joseph Proudhon famously declared, *"Property is robbery!"*[8] because, he claimed, if all people ought to be equal, then for one person to own more than another means that he or she took more than his or her fair share.

I'll address inequality in the next chapter, but suffice it to say for now that one thing Proudhon didn't see is that the consequences of taking away all private property would be disastrous. We can point to historical examples from the twentieth century, such as the Russian or Cuban revolutions or the so-called Cultural Revolution in China, to see vividly how such "equality" requires monstrous acts of violence, and even then cannot be achieved. In some cases the political order people rebelled against may have been truly unjust. But in every case the result was not an equalization of society but a new (and often worse) inequality, one purchased with the blood not only of tyrants but also of many innocent people.

On a less severe level, arguments against private property tend to overlook what economists call the tragedy of the commons. There are many dynamics involved, and not every solution boils down to private property, but the tragedy of the commons helps to illustrate some of the lost benefits if private property is taken away. The term can be traced to the early English economist William Forster Lloyd. At that time in England, in addition to private land, there were shared common areas for grazing cattle.

Sounds like a good idea, right? Shouldn't that benefit everyone? Unfortunately, it didn't always work out that way. He wrote,

> In an inclosed [i.e., privately owned] pasture, there is a point of saturation ... beyond which no prudent man will add to his stock. In a common, also, there is in like manner a point of saturation. But the position of the point in the two cases is obviously different. Were a number of adjoining pastures, already fully stocked, to be at once thrown open, and converted into one vast common, the position of the point of saturation would immediately be changed. The stock would be increased, and would be made to press much more forcibly against the means of subsistence.[9]

Why is this? Because now everyone has a larger field for their stock of cattle, but that field is shared. Thus, each person will want to get the most benefit possible out of the available grazing land, leading to overgrazing and ultimately hurting everyone. For Lloyd, like Malthus, this was important to demonstrate the problem of overpopulation. But its application goes beyond that (in hindsight) flawed motivation.

A more contemporary example may help to illustrate this: group work in schools. Four college students, Sally, Jack, Jill, and Tom, are assigned to work together on a group project for their Early Byzantine Basket Weaving Studies course. Their professor assigned the groups to include students of a variety of achievement levels, thus hoping to avoid all the A students' forming a group and leaving everyone else to struggle on their own. But this good intention has other unseen and negative effects that everyone who has been in this situation has experienced.

Imagine that the students' grades in the class break down as follows:

Student	Letter Grade	Grade Points
Sally	A	4.0
Jack	B	3.0
Jill	C	2.0
Tom	C	2.0
Group Average	B-	2.75

Sally is a good student, and she needs to maintain her A to keep her scholarships. Jack is a decent student and wants at least a B. It also turns out he has a crush on Jill. Jill wants to do better than a C, but she has really been struggling to understand Byzantine basket weaving. Tom could do better, but he only took the class because he heard it was an easy way to fulfill his history requirement. His philosophy is: "C's get degrees!"

The first group meeting seems to go well. Sally takes charge right away, paranoid about not getting an A. Jack volunteers to help Jill, and both of them are motivated to do better than their overall grade in the class. With Jack's extra effort to help her, Jill is able to do better than she would have on her own. So the amount of effort, measured in grade points, changes:

Student	Effort (in Grade Points)
Sally	4.0
Jack	3.5
Jill	2.5
Tom	2.0
Group Average	3.0

An average of 3.0 brings the expected group grade up to a B. That satisfies Jack, and Jill would be thrilled, which Jack also wants. This is an example of how community can be positive. Group ownership, even state ownership, is not always bad. We do need other people, after all. But Sally isn't happy with this result. She still needs an A.

Sally needs the total group effort to average at 4.0. So she calculates that even with Jack helping Jill, she needs to put forth double her normal effort to make that happen:

Student	Effort (in Grade Points)
Sally	8.0
Jack	3.5
Jill	2.5
Tom	2.0
Group Average	4.0

Unfortunately for Sally, however, her willingness to sacrifice for the group and double her already high-achieving effort does not go unnoticed by Tom. Tom only cares about not getting less than a C. And since these precise numbers are not actually known to the participants, it is unlikely that the calculation will turn out perfectly for Sally. In fact, Tom undermines her efforts when he realizes that now he doesn't need to do any work in order to get a C or better on the project.

Lacking any strong motivation, Tom makes up excuses for why he can't make it to future meetings. "I forgot I have ultimate Frisbee practice then," he says the first time. "I need to study for an exam in another class," he says the second time. The third time he just doesn't show up. In the end, he barely contributes, even arriving late on the day the group is supposed to present their project. So the end result looks like this:

Student	Effort (in Grade Points)
Sally	8.0
Jack	3.5
Jill	2.5
Tom	0
Group Average	3.5

A 3.5 turns out to be a B+. Jack and Jill try to comfort Sally—after all, the grade is better than either of them expected or hoped for—but Sally is red in the face. She confronts Tom after class, yelling at him for slacking off. Tom's response, however, is somewhat surprising: "Sally, you didn't want anyone else's input from the beginning. I could tell that you're a perfectionist. You didn't care about my suggestions anyway because you had to be in control. So I let you have what you wanted. Don't be mad at me."

Sally is now left conflicted. On the one hand, Tom should have contributed more to the group, but on the other hand, did her ambition actually encourage his idleness? Worse, because the group project is such a big part of students' overall grade in the class, now in order to keep her A she needs to beg her professor for extra credit. Her professor is annoyed by this but eventually relents. So Sally can still get her A, but she must further sacrifice what little social life she has to do it, even after already doubling her work on the group project.

This situation could have been even worse. Imagine if it turns out Jill has a crush on Jack too. They decide they don't care as much about their grades as they do about making out. Their contribution becomes minimal as well, and even with extra credit poor Sally can't get her A and loses her scholarships. When it comes to the commons, the self-interest of individuals tends to hurt others in unseen ways that go beyond the immediate effects, violating legal justice in their efforts and distributive justice in the outcome.

By contrast, if there had been no group project in the class, each person would have been responsible for his or her own grade. Jack could still help Jill study, and maybe her grade could still improve. But Sally would have to do a lot less work (and get to have a social life), and whether she keeps her A would be in her hands. Furthermore, Tom would actually need to put forth a C's worth of effort to get a C in the class. Student contributions are likely to be more equal, and results are likely to be more just. Perhaps paradoxically, the common good of student performance as a whole is more likely to be maximized by forgoing such group projects.

Now imagine that instead of students, we were talking about corporations: SallyCorp, Jack & Jill Enterprises, and Tom Industries. Some commons are unavoidable, such as air. No one owns the air. But everyone uses it and needs it. SallyCorp is an environmentally conscious company. It goes out of its way to reduce carbon emissions, wanting to reduce smog and contribute less to climate change. Jack & Jill Enterprises does a decent job, though they can't afford to try as hard as SallyCorp. If they did, they wouldn't make a profit and their business would fail. Tom Industries simply doesn't care about the air and dominates the market. So what if a few more children get asthma? So what if the sunset is obscured by smog? And as for climate change (if it is even real), no matter how much the business pollutes, its contribution is ultimately minimal. It's just one company, after all. The Economish term for this is a negative externality. It is a cost to society that the producer doesn't have to pay.

If these businesses are state owned, the goal may be simply to have a decent average of pollution between them. If that is the case, then the average might be fine under current practices. (Think of the B+ the student project got in the example above.) However, if each business is privately owned, the state might be more likely to evaluate each one individually. In response, it could institute a carbon tax and subsidy scheme. There are reasons to object to this kind of regulation even if someone cares about smog and climate change, but I can't get into that level of detail. I'll look at regulations more generally in the section on free markets in the next chapter.

In this arrangement companies like SallyCorp would get a subsidy to make up for the costs of being overachievers when it comes to reducing pollution. Jack & Jill Enterprises might do a little better too; they won't have to increase their costs to do so and can still stay in business. And Tom Industries will face an extra cost through the tax that will incentivize it to do better in reducing pollution and that will finance the subsidy to more carbon-conscious businesses in the meantime. Thus, private ownership is more likely to reduce pollution and benefit the environment.

This isn't just a conjecture. Somewhat oversimplifying, the economist Ronald Coase argued that "the best way to manage externalities (read pollution) is to have well-defined property rights."[10] Regulation isn't even needed for private property to benefit the environment. Think of things that private property *takes away* from the commons like land, water, and other natural resources. When these belong to private citizens, they have the freedom to use them as they please, but they also bear the consequences of abusing them. So there is a built-in motivation for treating them well. That's not everyone's land or water, it's *their* land or their water. Similarly, that's not everyone's oil or iron or timber, it's *their* oil or iron or timber. "Overgrazing" in these areas, to use Lloyd's example, becomes less likely.

Danish economist Lars Christensen, on his blog *The Market Monetarist*, tested Coase's theory by plotting a measure of property rights on one axis of a graph and environmental care on another,[11] as seen in figure 1 below:

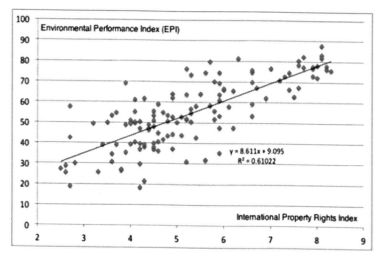

Figure 1

Now, for those who don't speak Math, don't worry. I can translate. This can be simplified as follows: The dots plot individual countries' actual scores on each index. The line shows that the relationship between them is generally positive. That is, as private property rights increase, so does environmental performance (and vice versa). Thus, the actual data we have backs up the theory we've explored.

There is one last consequence of what would happen without private property that I can't overlook. It is not so much environmental or economic as it is political. *Without private property, people cannot be free.* By "free" here, I mean the political idea of self-government or sovereignty. As I already noted, without private property, churches would be at the mercy of the state. But that is true for every other social sphere and private institution as well, from the family to sports teams to poker clubs to charities to schools to businesses. When people are allowed to own things, they gain sovereignty over them.

Abraham Kuyper would rightly remind us that ultimately God is the true owner of the world, and we are just his stewards. He's right. But private citizens would not even get to be stewards without private property. And as we've already noted, private property actually tends to increase private responsibility, i.e., good stewardship. It doesn't guarantee it, of course, and no doubt readers can think of countless real-world examples of all the Toms and Tom Industries of the world. But according to the data we have and the basic economic theory we've covered in this section, the general trend is overwhelmingly for the common good. The total absence of private property would be disastrous in more ways than one.

Profits

In a catechetical lecture in 2013, Pope Francis urged his audience to solidarity with the poor and marginalized. This is one of the most consistent and laudable emphases of his pontificate. But sometimes what is seen overshadows what is not seen. "If you break a computer it is a tragedy," said Francis,

> but poverty, the needs, the dramas of so many people end up becoming the norm. If on a winter's night, here nearby in Via Ottaviano, for example, a person dies, that is not news. If in so many parts of the world there are children who have nothing to eat, that's not news, it seems normal. It cannot be this way! Yet these things become the norm: that some homeless people die of cold on the streets is not news. In contrast, a ten point drop on the stock markets of some cities, is a tragedy.

To Francis, this is because "men and women are sacrificed to the idols of profit and consumption."[12] I would like to emphasize that what the pope sees is right. Profits should not be more important than people. Waste is bad stewardship. The plight of the poor deserves more regular media attention. Solidarity is a virtue. All of these things are true, but Francis—like many others—fails to see the good of profit.

There is a false dichotomy here between profits and poverty. Stock markets measure company value, which is related to profit but not the same, and people can idolize that. But what Francis doesn't see is that without profit companies go out of business, all of the people who work for them lose their jobs, and *poverty grows*. As Adam Smith put it, "it is only for the sake of profit that any man employs a capital in the support of industry"[13] in the first place. Without profit there is no industry, and without industry there are no jobs. Profits do not require our ignoring the poor. And the poor will continue to be poor without profits. Rightly understood, concern for the stock market may in fact be concern for the poor on a massive scale.

The answer to the question, "What if there were no profits?" requires us to think through all the things profits are used for. Profit is the leftover when revenues exceed expenses. If there is no profit, it means companies can't pay their bills. Through loans, startups will often be able to endure years without profits. This is often necessary. But if they never end up making profits, pretty soon the loans will come due and the money needed to pay them won't be there. Companies will need to sell capital to pay them, and if that is not enough they will need to file for bankruptcy to renegotiate their debts. In either case, the company is done, and everyone who works for it will soon be unemployed.

So the first thing profits are used for is simply to keep businesses alive. There are many more uses than that, however. A company could conceivably stay alive by breaking even, where revenues equal expenses. But with profits, the company can expand, hire more people, pay higher wages, and diversify its product line. Furthermore, profits are often also used to invest in *other* companies, for example through 401(k) programs. Typically both employers and employees contribute to them. Unless the employee chooses to invest only in government bonds (which can also be good for society), they will be using some of their income and some of the company's profit (now an expense) to contribute to other enterprises in an economy, making more products, more profits, and more jobs possible. As we've already seen, without profits, business would be impossible. And without business, there are no jobs. The alternative to profits is universal poverty. That is exactly what we can see in dystopian dictatorships like North Korea: the otherwise unseen effects of taking away both profits and private property. Same planet, same dimension.

Pope John Paul II approached the issue with a bit more nuance:

> The Church acknowledges the legitimate *role of profit* as an indication that a business is functioning well. When a firm makes a profit, this means that productive factors have been properly employed and corresponding human needs have been duly satisfied. But profitability is not the only indicator of a firm's condition. It is possible for the financial accounts to be in order, and yet for the people—who make up the firm's most valuable asset—to be humiliated and their dignity offended. Besides being morally inadmissible, this will eventually have negative repercussions on the firm's economic efficiency. In fact, the purpose of a business firm is not simply to make a profit, but is to be found in its very existence as a *community of persons* who in various ways are endeavouring to satisfy their basic needs, and who form a particular group at the service of the whole of society. Profit is a regulator of the life of a business, but it is not the only one; *other human and moral factors* must also be considered which, in the long term, are at least equally important for the life of a business.[14]

Here John Paul II sees all of the same concerns as Francis: solidarity with workers, people over profits, and so on. Yet he also sees the often-overlooked importance of profit. It is "an indication that a business is functioning well," and it "means that productive factors have been properly employed and corresponding human needs have been duly satisfied." Rightly sought and understood, profits are a good thing.

Theologically speaking, such wholesome profit is what happens when people fulfill the command to "be fruitful" (Gen. 1:28). Or as Adam Smith dryly put it, "The produce of industry is what it adds to the subject or materials upon which it is employed. In proportion as the value of this produce is great or small, so will likewise be the profits of the employer."[15] When people profit from the creation of new wealth, it is because they take the world God has given us and make something more of it for the good of others and for God's glory. It would be shameful to throw that away.

This brings me to one last point, however. It is not true that *all* profit is good. There are some people who profit in North Korea, after all: the government elites. But their profit mostly comes from hoarding the aid they receive and the little wealth the nation still produces. And they spend it on things like parades and festivities for their "Dear Leader" or for expanding their military, which do nothing to raise the standard of living for the vast majority of their citizens. On a similar but much smaller level, as we have already seen, individual companies can profit at the expense of society as well by take advantage of common resources. And we will see in the next chapter how they can also do so through subsidies, taxes, and regulations that favor them at the expense of everyone else.

Free Prices

At first glance the idea of free prices might sound like an oxymoron. Prices tell us when something isn't free, after all. Of course, that is not the sense in which free is being used here. The free in free prices indicates who gets to set prices. Are they the organic product of the interaction between ever-changing supply and demand? Or are they set by someone other than producers and consumers?

Probably the most common example of a price that people don't want to be free is the minimum wage. In a letter to Congress in 2014, thirty-three faith leaders in conjunction with Interfaith Worker Justice and Faith in Public Life expressed their support for raising the federal minimum wage in the United States. Rather than making an argument on prudential grounds and weighing the costs as well as the benefits, they expressed firm belief that the issue is a clear-cut matter of principle: "Driven by

Scripture's repeated admonitions against exploiting and oppressing workers, we believe that every job must enable those who work to support a family." They continue, "For the minimum wage to be moral and just, it must be a living family wage. A minimum wage that pays a full-time worker $290 a week is unjust in an economy as wealthy as ours."[16]

Who wouldn't want that, right? The way these leaders frame the issue, the person opposed to raising the minimum wage must want poor families to continue to struggle to support themselves or at least be ignorant of their plight. No alternatives, such as wage subsidies like earned income tax credits, are considered. Furthermore, any other position must be *immoral and unscriptural* according to the letter. These are serious charges. And they're incorrect.

First, economically speaking, fixing prices typically leads to one of two possible outcomes. If the price is fixed higher than what it would be if people were free to offer and accept or reject whatever prices they wanted, there will be surpluses, i.e., fewer items will be sold than had been made. If the price is set below that level, there will be shortages, i.e., supply will not be able to keep pace with demand, and people who want and can afford a product (and who may even *need* it) will not be able to get it. The point where supply freely meets demand is the equilibrium.

Applied to wages, the supply is labor. When a minimum wage is set higher than the equilibrium would be without it, there will be supply surpluses. What does that mean? That means some people who want to work won't be able to find a job. As we discussed in chapter 2, that especially means increased unemployment among youth (who typically don't have families to support and don't need "living wages" anyway) and low-skilled minority workers. Why? Because increasing the cost of labor means those costs need to be paid somehow. So employers can afford to hire fewer people. These workers especially need low-paying jobs to get the work experience they need to leverage for better paying jobs in the future. The jobs lost to minimum wages are some of the most crucial in an economy: They are the first step of the ladder of upward income mobility, and when those jobs are reduced that mobility slows.

In some cases companies will raise prices to cover the costs (causing inflation if widespread enough and either way hurting consumers). However, it also means that they will become pickier about who they hire. Since wages have gone up, more qualified people will suddenly be interested. While prejudice may be a factor, this hurts minority workers simply because, statistically, they tend to be less educated in general. Why would a coffee shop hire someone without a high school diploma when college graduates are now applying to be baristas?

Furthermore, more unemployment means more people who, through no fault of their own in this case, become dependent on state and other assistance that could otherwise be used for different social needs. So there is an additional opportunity cost attached to this problem. Economies lose the labor of people who would like to work, and resources that could have been channeled toward other causes are diverted to support them. Furthermore, national and state minimum wages, which focus on income inequality instead of consumption disparities, cannot account for differences in cost of living among different localities and violate the principle of subsidiarity by usurping what would be better handled by local governments (or no governments).

Keen readers will likely have noticed the seemingly radical implication of this, however. Am I suggesting that we shouldn't have a national minimum wage at all? Basically, yes. But it isn't radical. Sweden, Denmark, Iceland, Norway, and Switzerland have no national minimum wages but still enjoy high standards of living.[17] In fact, the "Nordic model" of the first four is sometimes appealed to as the ideal by the same people who want to raise the minimum wage in the United States.[18] But if they can have what they want without hurting the youth and low-skilled minorities by raising the minimum wage, why not let it go? Why not give workers and unions the sovereignty to freely negotiate wages with employers? Shouldn't business and labor be their own sovereign social spheres?[19]

"Blessed is he who considers the poor," says the psalmist (Ps. 41:1). Considering the poor, however, requires seeing more than the apparent, immediate gains of policies intended to help them. In the case of low-wage workers, the question should be how to reduce the cost of living and extend the ladder of mobility, not how to raise the first rung of that ladder to a height that many cannot reach. The reason companies in these countries don't just reduce wages to oppressive lows is because people will simply refuse to work if the wage offered is too low. Wages are naturally regulated by the free preferences of workers. So another way to look at it is that minimum wages aren't bad, as long as they fall below the lowest equilibrium point. But that also would make them moot, the virtual equivalent of not having a minimum at all.

The problems with price fixing don't end there, however. Wages are just one example. But free prices are an essential part of a larger competitive process in markets. The economist Friedrich Hayek described this as a discovery procedure.[20] To briefly summarize, when an enterprise, say Company X, produces a product (doodads), its marketing team generally does some research to get an idea of what price people are willing to pay for doodads before mass producing them. This is vital because Company X must have some idea ahead of time, if only an intuition, that they will be able to recoup their costs and make a profit. If not, as we now know, Company X might go bust.

Furthermore, once the doodads are on the market, Company X will soon discover how well they judged. If it turns out that they overestimated demand, they will have to adjust the price in order to try to minimize their losses as much as possible. If it turns out that they underestimated demand, then that is a good problem. Stores will run out of stock in their product for a while, but now they will know that they can price the next version of doodads at an even higher level while still satisfying demand, increasing profit, and thus investing in future expansion. Additionally, if a competitor makes a superior product, such as Whiz-Bang™ doodads, demand for Company X's ordinary doodads will decrease, forcing them, once again, to adjust prices. And so on.

Free prices convey information and act as an important feedback mechanism. Specifically, they show us the meeting point between producers' costs and the subjective preferences of consumers. Both of these can and do change. Without free prices, however, adjustments cannot be made fast enough to account for these changes. The competitive procedure becomes impossible, all of its benefits are lost, and waste increases.

Fixing prices is not the only way to undermine free prices, however. Anything that separates costs from consumption does this as well. What do I mean by this? Look at higher education prices in the United States. Since the 1980s, the price of higher education has greatly outpaced economic growth and inflation. As the Obama administration noted in 2013, "The average tuition at a public four-year college has increased by more than 250 percent over the past three decades, while incomes for typical families grew by only 16 percent."[21]

What they didn't seem to see is that one of the major reasons for this is federally backed student loans, which were greatly expanded in the 1980s, a shift away from need-based grants. As a result, the ordinary calculation of risk was ignored, since nearly any student could now qualify for these loans. As more and more students paid in future, rather than present, money through debt, the price of tuition ballooned. No matter how much costs rose, loans kept being issued, and elders kept telling students that they should do whatever it takes to get a college degree as a golden ticket to the middle class. The common law promulgated here is that if a student wants to succeed in life, he or she must get a degree. But just like with Willy Wonka's chocolate factory, people are increasingly discovering that not everyone who gets this golden ticket ends up coming out happy in the end.

Why did costs rise? Because they were ultimately hidden by the loans. Of course, people saw the price tag. But when they didn't have to come up with the money ahead of time, they were more likely to agree to pay the price. In conjunction with the increased push for higher education in general over these years, regardless of one's major or employment prospects afterward, demand for higher education artificially soared, and so did prices. Even today, the demand for higher education remains fairly inelastic, but as fewer employers are impressed by bachelor's degrees (at least in certain majors), a time may come when students and parents start to think twice before signing up for college. If they do, it could result in a wide-reaching economic crisis by causing many schools to become insolvent. In the meantime, an intervention intended to help those who couldn't afford college has made degrees more expensive for everyone by undermining the free determination of prices.

Money

In the apostle Paul's first epistle to Timothy, he includes a warning about money:

> Those who desire to be rich fall into temptation and a snare, and into many foolish and harmful lusts which drown men in destruction and perdition. For the love of money is a root of all kinds of evil, for which some have strayed from the faith in their greediness, and pierced themselves through with many sorrows. But you, O man of God, flee these things and pursue righteousness, godliness, faith, love, patience, gentleness. (1 Tim. 6:9–11)

This is often erroneously summarized as "money is the root of all evil," but that is clearly not what Paul said. It is the "desire to be rich" and "the love of money" that are the problem. Why? Because such an outlook confuses a means with an end. If treating *a person* as a means to an end is a sin (and it is), so, too, is treating *an object* as an end in itself. When that object is money or riches, that is the definition of greed. But ignoring an object's nature is surely a mistake as well. So it is important to understand what money is, how it works, and why that matters.

Couldn't we do away with this problem if we just didn't have money? Certainly, if money itself really was the "root of all evil," then abolishing it would be the most moral thing to do. However, if the problem, just as it was in the garden, is not the object but the desire for it, then the solution to greed is a matter of the salvation of our souls. We need deliverance from the vices and sins that hold us down, which for Christians is what the gospel is for, not laws.

What people don't often see is that the alternative to money is a barter economy. While this is sometimes romanticized, it would be a mistake to think it is better. For one thing, Walter Eucken insisted that "even in the barter economy there may still be a scale of reckoning, which may be cattle or a unit of some standard good, without there being a generally recognized means of exchange—that is, money."[22] So even without money, people naturally adopt some money-like "scale of reckoning." Money is just an advancement on that.

Eucken's analysis gives us a clear picture of what money is really for:

> The exchange value of a good is a definite quantity because and only because a scale of reckoning is being used. If wool were being exchanged against flax, tin, bread, labour, and other goods, without the use of a scale of reckoning, it would exchange at as many different rates as there were goods. If copper becomes the scale of reckoning and a unit of copper the unit of account, then all the exchange relations will be described in terms of copper and therefore become comparable.[23]

What money allows us to do is to compare the economic value of all sorts of different goods in an economy. Remember, economic value is distinct from moral or artistic value. It represents the subjective preferences of everyone in an economy. That information is conveyed through prices, and in large economies prices are measured in money.

Why is this a good thing? Because money enables us to portion out our resources in ways we otherwise could not. It helps us be better stewards of God's world. If a farmer, Maggie, has a cow in a barter economy, she must accept a trade in one or a combination of other goods, such as chickens, corn, horseshoes, and so on. But then, if she takes it, she is stuck with those goods. She can try to trade again, and eventually get to a point where she is able to meet most of her needs, but it will take a lot of time and haggling. In our modern, super-connected, hyper-fast, global economies, that is time people simply do not have. The invention of money was an important advancement in human civilization.

Now imagine that Maggie has a cow in a monetary economy. She sells her cow for the best price she can find, and receives that price in money. With that money, she can then go and buy all the things she needs and can afford. She isn't stuck exchanging a lasso for some turnips with the hope that she can then exchange the turnips for something she actually wants and needs. (My choice of goods in this example betrays the fact that my idea of farming is unrealistically shaped by Western films, *Little House on the Prairie*, and that Oregon Trail computer game. Bear with me.) Now, Maggie can't cut a chicken into parts and keep the gizzard with the expectation that someone will be willing to trade two apple pies for that gizzard later. Similarly, if she tried to pay her workers in chicken gizzards, they'd likely say with American singer-songwriter and Nobel Laureate Bob Dylan, "I ain't gonna work on Maggie's farm no more."[24] But thankfully, in a monetary economy, she can sell a chicken for some money and then use the money to buy any variety of things she wants or needs, whenever she needs them. (The Economish term for this is "fungibility," which is fun to say.) Money serves a vital human need by helping economic exchange better serve other human needs.

Most people, however, are not anarchists or Marxists who actually desire the abolition of money. What is a much bigger problem is policymakers' misunderstanding the nature of money in other ways. In particular, every so often a government forgets (or purposefully ignores) the fact that money, just like every other economic good, is subject to supply and demand. Early modern Spanish kings, for example, were advised to debase their currency. But the result was simply that people, including the king, ended up needing more of it to buy the same things.[25] People value a coin of 10 percent gold a lot less than one of 100 percent gold. If demand drops, supply must increase to keep up.

While most modern currencies are no longer tied to gold, they can still be debased, arguably more easily. All a government needs to do is print more of it (or the digital equivalent). By increasing the supply, the value of the currency decreases—supply and demand. This is one source of "inflation," which is the Economish word for how prices increase as the money supply increases or inflates. As a result, the value of the money decreases.

To some extent, all modern governments do a little of this. Deflation—reduction in the money supply—is feared because it would mean that debts would increase. Why? Because if I take out a loan for one thousand dollars today, but the value of the dollar increases, then the thousand dollars I will use to pay that loan in the future will be worth more. The real value of the debt has increased, even though the number of dollars owed stays the same. By contrast, and for the same reason, inflation encourages debt (and, if too high, discourages saving). If the money I use to pay back a debt will be worth less than the money I get at the time of the loan, then I'm getting a deal. Banks compensate for inflation and the risk that I won't be able to repay the debt through interest.

So a little inflation can help ward off deflation and encourage investment since people are more likely to take out loans. Deflation isn't the only thing to worry about though. If inflation gets out of hand, people will stop valuing that currency at all. This happened in Germany in the early twentieth century. This happened in Russia toward the end of the Soviet era. And more recently, this happened in the nightmarish failure of the Venezuelan government's "twenty-first century socialism." Same planet, same dimension. In Venezuela, they literally couldn't print money fast enough to pay their debts, which, incidentally, contributed to the hyperinflation in the first place. They tried to shut down currency exchanges to force people to use Venezuelan money (otherwise how would they fix prices?), but it didn't work. No matter what tyrannical restrictions people implement, supply and demand are simply facts of our social life.

If a currency fails through inflation, people will find some other unit of reckoning: cigarettes, grain, metals, or something else. The disadvantage all of these have, however, is that not everyone universally wants them, and in many cases they are much harder to protect and store than money. Some of them may even be perishable, making long-term saving impossible. The collapse of Venezuela's formerly advanced economy to a barter system has meant widespread hunger, crime, and poverty. A barter system can't support a society that large. Venezuela's monetary system collapsed by its violating private property rights, fixing prices, demonizing profits, and debasing its currency, among other dystopian measures. The last straw was a sudden dip in oil prices, but many other oil-dominated economies survived when Venezuela's did not. As Dany Bahar and Miguel Angel Santos put it for the Brookings Institution at the time, "Venezuela's current crisis was completely preventable. In fact, it is the consequence of almost two decades of irresponsible policies."[26] Unfortunately those who foresaw the coming collapse were ignored.

Without a stable currency—one with low and steady inflation—commerce breaks down. People seek to get rid of money as soon as they get it, only further contributing to the inflation. Why keep a dollar today if it will only be worth a dime tomorrow? So people stop saving. Banks stop issuing loans. Foreign investment dries up. Trade disappears. The wealthy migrate. Vital consumer goods go missing. Poverty and hunger grow. The lesson: Money matters, and it is not exempt from the laws of our economic life. We need it, and we need to treat it right. It is not an end in itself, as the greedy think, but it is also not something without its own internal laws and properties. These laws are what make it an asset to the common good, and ignoring them damages the general welfare.[27]

Discussion Questions

1. What does it mean to be a good economist, according to Bastiat? How can the economic way of thinking benefit you beyond even the economic aspects of your life?

2. What if you didn't have private property? How would your own life be different if you didn't have control over the things you own ... or own them at all?

3. What are all the ways in your own life that you seek profit? What did Jesus mean when he asked, "For what will it profit a man if he gains the whole world, and loses his own soul?" (Mark 8:36) How can we put pursuing the material profit we need to provide for our needs in harmony with the spiritual profit Jesus commends that outweighs the whole world?

4. What's the problem with governments fixing prices? What is lost when we don't allow prices to result from the free interaction of supply and demand?

5. Isn't money the root of all evil? How can a person respect the good nature of money without falling into greed?

Notes

1. Lionel Robbins, *An Essay on the Nature & Significance of Economic Science* (London: MacMillan, 1932), 15.

2. Ambrose of Milan, *De Officiis Ministrorum*, 1.12 in *NPNF*² 10:9.

3. Ambrose, *De Officiis*, 1.12, 8.

4. Frédéric Bastiat, "That Which Is Seen and That Which Is Not Seen," in Bastiat, *The Bastiat Collection*, 2nd ed. (Auburn, AL: Ludwig von Mises Institute, 2007), 1.

5. For a recent example of this, see David Bentley Hart, "Christ's Rabble: The First Christians Were Not Like Us," *Commonweal* 143, no. 16 (September 27, 2016): 18–21, https://www.commonwealmagazine.org/christs-rabble. See also my response to Hart: Dylan Pahman, "On Wealth and the Bible, The First Christians Were Not Like David Bentley Hart," *Public Discourse*, October 3, 2016, http://www.thepublicdiscourse.com/2016/10/17950/.

6. See, for example, "Jailed Joseph: China's Crackdown on Christian Churches," *The Daily Beast*, May 8, 2016, http://www.thedailybeast.com/articles/2016/05/08/china-s-crackdown-on-christian-churches.html.

7. Gerard Berghoef and Lester DeKoster, *The Deacons Handbook: A Manual of Stewardship* (Grand Rapids: Christian's Library Press, 1980), 44.

8. P. J. Proudhon, *The Works of P. J. Proudhon*, vol. 1: *What Is Property?*, trans. Benjamin R. Tucker (Princeton, MA: Benjamin R. Tucker, 1876), 12.

9. W. F. Lloyd, *Two Lectures on the Checks to Population* (Oxford: S. Collingwood, 1833), 31–32.

10. Lars Christensen, "Coase Was Right," *The Market Monetarist*, December 1, 2015, https://marketmonetarist.com/2015/12/01/coase-was-right-the-one-graph-version/.

11. Christensen, "Coase Was Right."

12. "Pope at Audience: Counter a Culture of Waste with Solidarity," *Vatican Radio*, May 6, 2013, http://en.radiovaticana.va/storico/2013/06/05/pope_at_audience_counter_a_culture_of_waste_with_solidarity/en1-698604.

13. Adam Smith, *An Inquiry into the Nature and Causes of the Wealth of Nations*, vol. 1, Glasgow Edition of the Works of Adam Smith, vol. 2 (Indianapolis: LibertyClassics, 1981), 455. Henceforth: *Wealth of Nations*.

14. Pope John Paul II, encyclical letter *Centesimus Annus*, May 1, 1991, 35, http://w2.vatican.va/content/john-paul-ii/en/encyclicals/documents/hf_jp-ii_enc_01051991_centesimus-annus.html.

15. Adam Smith, *Wealth of Nations*, 455.

16. This letter was formerly available at http://www.faithinpubliclife.org/wp-content/uploads/2014/04/Religious-sign-on_MinWage_National.pdf, but has since been removed. This paragraph is adapted from an essay I wrote on the just wage. See Dylan Pahman, "Giving the Just Wage Its Due," *Acton Commentary*, May 28, 2014, http://www.acton.org/pub/commentary/2014/05/28/giving-just-wage-its-due.

17. See Claire Boyte-White, "5 Developed Countries without Minimum Wages," *Investopedia*, August 5, 2015, http://www.investopedia.com/articles/investing/080515/5-developed-countries-without-minimum-wages.asp.

18. See Dylan Pahman, "Sorry Bernie: Scandinavia Isn't Socialist. You Must Be Thinking of France," *The Stream*, May 19, 2016, https://stream.org/sorry-bernie-scandinavia-isnt-socialist/.

19. This was Kuyper's view on the matter as well. See Abraham Kuyper, "Manual Labor (1889)," in *Abraham Kuyper: a Centennial Reader*, ed. James D. Bratt (Grand Rapids: Eerdmans, 1998), 231–54.

20. See Friedrich Hayek, "Competition as a Discovery Procedure," trans. Marcellus S. Snow, *The Quarterly Journal of Austrian Economics* 5, no. 3 (Fall 2002): 9–23.

21. Office of the Press Secretary, "FACT SHEET on the President's Plan to Make College More Affordable: A Better Bargain for the Middle Class," The White House, August 22, 2013, https://www.whitehouse.gov/the-press-office/2013/08/22/fact-sheet-president-s-plan-make-college-more-affordable-better-bargain-.

22. Walter Eucken, *The Foundations of Economics: History and Theory in the Analysis of Economic Reality*, trans. T. W. Hutchinson (Chicago: University of Chicago Press, 1951), 159.

23. Eucken, *The Foundations of Economics*, 160.

24. Bob Dylan, "Maggie's Farm," *Bringing It All Back Home* (Burbank: Warner Bros., 1965), track 3.

25. See Juan de Mariana, *A Treatise on the Alteration of Money*, trans. P. T. Brannan, Sources in Early Modern Economics, Ethics, and Law (1609; repr., Grand Rapids: Christian's Library Press, 2011).

26. Dany Bahar and Miguel Angel Santos, "Should Venezuela Seek International Assistance? Ways Out of the Economic and Humanitarian Crisis," *Brookings*, June 2, 2016, https://www.brookings.edu/blog/future-development/2016/06/02/should-venezuela-seek-international-assistance-ways-out-of-the-economic-and-humanitarian-crisis/.

27. This section on money is a revised version of an essay I wrote on the subject. See Dylan Pahman, "Why Money Matters," *Religion & Liberty* (Fall 2016): 6–8.

5

Inequality, Equality, and Freedom

*Liberty ... is the delicate fruit of a mature
civilization; and scarcely a century has passed
since nations, that knew the meaning of the term,
resolved to be free. In every age its progress has
been beset by its natural enemies, by ignorance
and superstition, by lust of conquest and by love
of ease, by the strong man's craving for power,
and the poor man's craving for food.*

—Lord Acton[1]

Introduction

In the case of inequality, an excellent "What if?" already exists in
the form of the 1961 short story "Harrison Bergeron" by American
novelist Kurt Vonnegut, Jr. The story begins as follows:

> The year was 2081, and everybody was finally equal. They
> weren't only equal before God and the law. They were equal
> every which way. Nobody was smarter than anybody else.
> Nobody was better looking than anybody else. Nobody was
> stronger or quicker than anybody else. All this equality
> was due to the 211th, 212th, and 213th Amendments to
> the Constitution, and to the unceasing vigilance of agents
> of the United States Handicapper General.

> Some things about living still weren't quite right, though. April, for instance, still drove people crazy by not being springtime. And it was in that clammy month that the H-G men took George and Hazel Bergeron's fourteen-year-old son, Harrison, away.
>
> It was tragic, all right, but George and Hazel couldn't think about it very hard. Hazel had a perfectly average intelligence, which meant she couldn't think about anything except in short bursts. And George, while his intelligence was way above normal, had a little mental handicap radio in his ear. He was required by law to wear it at all times. It was tuned to a government transmitter. Every twenty seconds or so, the transmitter would send out some sharp noise to keep people like George from taking unfair advantage of their brains.[2]

The story goes on to detail an absurd ballet the Bergerons watch on television, where the dancers wear masks to cover their beauty, weights to impair their movement, and for two of them, little mental handicap radios in their ears like George. Vonnegut hints throughout the hilarity of the story that despite the efforts of the Handicapper General, inequality can never be completely eliminated, and there is something deep within the human heart that would manage to mourn any such totalitarian attempt.

There is also, unfortunately, something deep within the human heart that disdains all inequality. Now, of course, some inequality deserves to be disdained. Jim Crow laws, written in the name of equality "separate but equal," created a regime of racial inequality, the tragic legacy of which the United States still lives with today. But there are many wonderful ways in which human beings are different from one another—and in that sense unequal—that we should not do away with. Vonnegut's story draws that out.

Another story that gets at this problem comes, once again, from Genesis. Adam and Eve made a big mistake (to put it lightly), but the severity of their sin becomes much clearer in the story of their two sons, Cain and Abel. The story goes as follows:

> Now Abel was a keeper of sheep, but Cain was a tiller of the ground. And in the process of time it came to pass that

Cain brought an offering of the fruit of the ground to the Lord. Abel also brought of the firstborn of his flock and of their fat. And the Lord respected Abel and his offering, but He did not respect Cain and his offering. And Cain was very angry, and his countenance fell.

So the Lord said to Cain, "Why are you angry? And why has your countenance fallen? If you do well, will you not be accepted? And if you do not do well, sin lies at the door. And its desire is for you, but you should rule over it." (Gen. 4:2–7)

Poor Cain. He's like a biblical Rodney Dangerfield; he gets no respect. We don't know exactly what he did wrong up to this point, but look at what he did right: He was a tiller of the ground! That's *exactly* what, according to Genesis 2, God created humanity to do. Or it is if the passage is taken literally anyway. Abel seems to have adopted a more creative hermeneutic to come up with animal husbandry. And God rewarded that creativity.

Cain is upset that his offering is not received equally with Abel's. He sees it as unfair. I must admit that I've always felt for him. There is much left unsaid in this story, which makes a great deal of room for empathy. Cain probably worked really hard, and as we've already pointed out, he was doing exactly what God had told humanity to do. Why the tough love?

Theologically, one lesson to learn here is that our deeds don't, of themselves, put God in our debt. Our relationship with him doesn't work that way. This is a lesson people in the Bible have to learn again and again, and it is a lesson people all throughout the history of salvation have had to learn again and again. It's a lesson I have to learn again and again in my own life. God said to Moses, "I will be gracious to whom I will be gracious, and I will have compassion on whom I will have compassion" (Ex. 33:19). I don't think the point of this is that God is fickle or arbitrary. Rather it is that he has his own standards and motivations that though necessarily just (for God is good and cannot be unjust) may seem unclear to us. It was, at least, unclear to Cain.

God offers Cain encouragement: "If you do well, will you not be accepted?" But how does Cain respond? "Now Cain talked with Abel his brother," says the Scripture. Oh good! Maybe Cain was getting some pointers from Abel. "And it came to pass, when they were in the field, that Cain rose up against Abel his brother and killed him" (Gen. 4:8). Whoops ... maybe not. Many of the ways of God may be inscrutable, but I think Cain knew, just as his parents had, that he made the wrong choice. Instead of conquering the sin growing from anger and desire in his heart, as God had cautioned him to do, Cain gave in to it in the most tragic way.

We face this same temptation in our economic lives today. Through envy—anger and grief over the good fortune of others—we lash out against other people. We may not be murderous like Cain, but the motivation is the same. Both desire for equality when it isn't merited *and* desire for inequality in places it does not belong threaten our freedom, diminish our ability to be truly fruitful stewards of God's world, and increase suffering and poverty. We see this problem in complaints over international trade, the benefits of technology, direct indictments of all economic inequality, or circumventions of the rule of law. Getting inequality and equality right is necessary for free markets, and free markets are necessary if we want to increase human flourishing and serve the common good. What happens if we don't get these things right? What happens if we don't have free markets? That's what we'll examine in this chapter.

Trade

In the 1990 film *Back to the Future Part III*, there is a scene in which cool kid Marty McFly (Michael J. Fox) and his inventor friend "Doc" Brown (Christopher Lloyd) are trying to fix Doc's time machine. Doc made the machine out of a car in 1985, and Marty inadvertently got sent back to 1955 while driving it. (I hate it when that happens!) Long story short, two movies later Marty and Doc are still trying to get him back to the future. In this particular scene, what's important is that this isn't the 1985 Doc but the 1955 Doc. He pulls a busted circuit out of the machinery and remarks to Marty, "No wonder this circuit failed. It says, 'Made in Japan.'" Marty responds, "What do you mean, Doc? All the best stuff is made in Japan." "Unbelievable!" Doc declares.

What if we didn't have international trade? In the 1980s and early 1990s there was a huge Buy American movement. Dana Frank captures the spirit of the time in her book of the same name: "The scene was like something out of a Batman cartoon. The first man lifted the sledgehammer, planted his feet wide apart, sighted over his left shoulder, and THWACK! sank it deep into the car with a grunt of pleasure. The crowd roared." She continues to explain what motivated this scene:

> The object of their aggression was a Toyota, its assailants members of the United Auto Workers [UAW] at a union picnic in the 1980s.... [E]mblematic of Buy American campaigns by the 1980s was the image of an unemployed auto worker in Detroit smashing a Japanese car. Autoworkers' hostility to Japanese imports captured the public imagination in the 1980s and early '90s, carrying the Buy American idea to the forefront of popular culture.[3]

So as not to paint a one-dimensional picture, it should be noted, as Frank points out, that "not everyone in the labor movement embraced nationalism."[4] The important point here is simply the picture that she paints. Marty's comment in *Back to the Future Part III* wasn't just a fun poke at how times had changed since the 1950s, it offered a subtle critique of the Buy American fad: In the future, Japan makes good products that Americans want and are used to purchasing. Anyone opposed must not have actually driven a Toyota vehicle or listened to a Sony Walkman or played a Nintendo video game. I wish I could say that we've put those Buy American days behind us, but economic nationalism has risen in recent years on both the political right and left all across the world. Unbelievable!

Many people still seem to think that the world would be a better place if the industries of their own nation were protected through subsidies and tariff taxes on imports. They are envious of the success of others and believe that that success has come at their expense. Often, just like at the UAW picnic, trade gets blamed for the decline of industries that used to provide abundant middle class jobs, especially manufacturing. Who would support that?

Well, I would. Moreover, I think I *ought to* because I believe that economics is a real science and that Christians (and people in general) have a duty to help the poor and transform the resources of our world to fruitfully produce wealth to serve human needs. Trade helps us do that better. We cannot be good stewards without it.

Imagine you are able to travel back in time to the 1980s. Same planet, different dimension, perhaps. Then imagine that you have an iPhone; you drop it and it breaks. Oh no! Who could fix such an advanced contraption in such a comparatively primitive time? Why, Doc Brown, of course! (Also, pretend the *Back to the Future* series was a documentary.) So you take your broken iPhone to the Doc. He's amazed at the technology. Opening it up, he finds the busted circuit. And what does he say? "No wonder this circuit failed. It says, 'Made in China.'" How would you respond? My response would be the same as Marty's: "What do you mean, Doc? All the best stuff is made in China." Unbelievable? I hope not.

Why does anybody trade anything? We've already covered this in chapter 3. Trade is a synonym for exchange, and people only exchange when they value what they are getting more than what they are giving. In this way, exchange benefits both people involved.

Trade also represents something else that we covered before: the division of labor. We saw the division of labor in Adam Smith's pin factory or in the making of this book. Trade is just the division of labor on an international scale. Remember how much more productive the pin factory was when the process was broken down into different steps, and different people were each assigned a different task? That's what happens with trade.

To explain this, we can go back to Smith. He illustrates this idea by reference to a smaller microcosm:

> To give the monopoly of the home-market to the produce of domestic industry, in any particular art or manufacture, is in some measure to direct private people in what manner they ought to employ their capitals, and must, in almost all cases, be either a useless or a hurtful regulation. If the produce of domestic can be brought there as cheap as that of foreign industry, the regulation is evidently useless. If it cannot, it must generally be hurtful. It is the maxim

of every prudent master of a family never to attempt to make at home what it will cost him more to make than to buy. The taylor does not attempt to make his own shoes, but buys them of the shoemaker. The shoemaker does not attempt to make his own clothes, but employs a taylor. The farmer attempts to make neither the one nor the other, but employs those different artificers. All of them find it for their interest to employ their whole industry in a way in which they have some advantage over their neighbours, and to purchase with a part of its produce, or what is the same thing, with the price of a part of it, whatever else they have occasion for.[5]

If a person can grasp Smith's point here, it isn't a big leap to see why international trade is actually a good thing, despite its growing unpopularity. The farmer says, "Why should I make shoes or clothes? I'm much better at growing crops and have little time left for anything else." So also, why make in the United States what can be made better in Japan or China or Mexico?

Now, the point isn't that we should all be unemployed and happy about it. The point is that sometimes we should be employed differently. As part of God's creation, we are subject to change, and that includes our economies. Just as we can die and rise daily, so can they. Many automobile factories in the United States were refitted to produce tanks, bombs, and airplanes during World War II. But when cheaper cars came from Japan forty years later, no one seems to have had enough imagination to ask themselves the most logical question, "What else could we make in these factories?" Instead, they held on to making cars as long as they could ... until they couldn't.

The Economish term for this concept is "comparative advantage." In the 1950s, 1960s, and 1970s, American companies had a comparative advantage at making cars. Then, throughout the 1980s, most of them lost that advantage. Smith helps us understand this as well:

> Though for want of such regulations the society should never acquire the proposed manufacture, it would not, upon that account, necessarily be the poorer in any one period of its duration. In every period of its duration its

whole capital and industry might still have been employed, though upon different objects, in the manner that was most advantageous at the time.[6]

We could have protected the American auto industry—and in some ways people tried—but we would only have done so to our own detriment. Furthermore, by resisting the changes in the industry for so long, rather than actively adapting to them, the negative effects on the American worker were likely amplified. That said, other unforeseen changes, such as the rise of Silicon Valley, also made up for the losses, inspiring more young adults to aspire to be computer engineers, graphic designers, programmers, and web developers rather than factory workers. The resources of our economy have since been better employed.

It is sometimes easier to get this when the example doesn't have any personal, emotional ties, as the American auto industry might for many readers. For a more remote example, Smith talks about why it would be a bad idea to make wine in Scotland:

> By means of glasses, hotbeds, and hot walls, very good grapes can be raised in Scotland, and very good wine too can be made of them at about thirty times the expence for which at least equally good can be brought from foreign countries. Would it be a reasonable law to prohibit the importation of all foreign wines merely to encourage the making of claret and burgundy in Scotland?[7]

Here we see again how the price system conveys valuable information. It told Adam Smith that making wine in Scotland would be a bad idea. It could be done, but the resources used to do it could be better and more profitably used on other things (like making scotch). Maybe the farmer could make her own shoes and clothes but probably only at the cost of growing fewer or lower quality crops. The lost profit in crops could have given the farmer enough money to buy more and better shoes and clothes as well as to meet other needs. In the same way, movements for localism and nationalism often actually hurt the localities and nations they seek to protect. Which brings up another thing people don't often see: Localism is just small-scale nationalism. The logic is the same, and the flaws are the same.

Another problem with economic nationalism is that it denies the essential dependency of all human people on one another. We need each other, and trade is one way in which people from all over the world provide for each other's needs. In fact, through globalization—the rapid increase in the velocity of travel and communication in the modern era—it is nearly impossible to turn back the clock on trade. One of the consequences of globalization is further economic integration. Not every component of an iPhone is made in China, for example, and Toyota and other foreign companies have factories in the United States. As of 2011, 80 percent of the parts used to build the popular Toyota Camry and Honda Accord models were manufactured in the United States, while 75 percent of the Chevy Malibu and 20 percent of the Ford Fusion were made here.[8] The reality of integration and interdependence is far more complex than nationalists make it out to be.

Trade is simply the international division of labor. It is global economic cooperation. Any given doodad in my house may contain components from five different countries. And everything that is traded needs to be shipped, which adds even more jobs. The Chinese aren't delivering iPhones to people's homes via long-range rocket or drone or carrier pigeon. People in every country in the world make their livings through the shipping industry. So to talk of "shipping jobs overseas," as often is the case (especially in election years), ironically misses the economic gains in shipping itself, not to mention every other aspect of economic reality it misses. Artificially keeping jobs of any given industry in one's country means a reduction in other jobs and other uses of resources that undoubtedly amount to a greater opportunity cost than the benefits to the protected industry. It thus unjustly serves the interest of a few at the expense of the many, not only abroad but at home as well. International trade is in the national interest. Nations are not atomistic individuals either.

In addition to all of this, less trade means more expensive goods (because resources are less efficiently used), thus hurting consumers. And if other nations respond by raising tariffs and effectively blocking exports from one's country, that means the loss of whole markets of potential consumers for the goods that a nation has a comparative advantage to make. In the case of China, that's more than one billion people. How would losing those potential consumers help American producers? The answer, of course, is that it wouldn't.

Technology

I, for one, welcome our new robot overlords. Well, not really—mainly because we don't actually face the threat of robot or computer overlords like Skynet (from the *Terminator* film series) anytime soon. And thankfully, neo-Luddites—those who argue for rejecting various modern technologies—are relatively few these days. Robot envy is not as common as envy of other nations. Nevertheless, the Luddites are not entirely absent, and less extreme but no less incorrect adherents, such as the novelist and poet Wendell Berry,[9] still exert considerable influence in some circles. In reality, however, technological progress has meant progress in human flourishing.

To answer the Luddites, first we must acknowledge that there is truth to what is seen. People see workers losing their jobs due to technology. When that happens (and it does), Christians and other people of good will should not be indifferent.

However, not *all* people who complain about the loss of manufacturing jobs see even this. The economic nationalists who oppose trade clearly do not. According to economist Ben Casselman, "In 1994 there were 3.5 million more Americans working in manufacturing than in retail. Today, those numbers have almost exactly reversed, and the gap is widening." He continues to note, however, that manufacturing production in the United States is still quite strong, having more than recovered since the 2008 recession. At the same time, manufacturing jobs have not increased proportionally with that production.[10] Why? In part because of technology. Despite their smaller numbers and the relative unpopularity of their cause, the neo-Luddites have a better case to make than the economic nationalists.

But it still isn't a good case. Yes, there are real losses that come from new technology—particularly in the short term—lost jobs. For example, a classic case of technological creative destruction, to use economist Joseph Schumpeter's term, is the newspaper business. According to Ken Doctor, "Newsroom jobs dropped 10.4 percent—down to 32,900 full-time journalists at nearly 1,400 U.S. dailies, 2014 over 2013."[11] 2015 was worse. As one Pew Report noted, "2015 was perhaps the worst year for newspapers since the Great Recession and its immediate aftermath. Daily circulation fell by 7%, the most since 2010, while advertising revenue at publicly traded newspaper companies fell by 8%, the most since 2009."[12]

While print books are actually keeping up quite well with ebooks, fewer and fewer people are getting their news from actual newspapers anymore. More and more readers are getting their news from online sources instead, and many formerly successful papers took too long to adjust and adjusted poorly. This means that the companies that supplied paper, ink, and any other aspect of the printing process have suffered losses too. Many traditional newspapers have cut back on their circulation and cut back on employment and pay, if not shut down business altogether.

What goes unseen? Online publication has exploded. Every website needs a web designer and manager. Every publication, regardless of the medium, needs editors. And, of course, more publications mean more opportunities for authors. These opportunities may be lower pay than what journalists used to start with, but they offer a foot in the door that for many may have been unavailable. More journalists and other writers can get real experience writing earlier in their careers, and they can leverage that experience and the connections they've made to move up the ladder of mobility. When people compare how things are to how things were, they complain about the lower pay rates, failing to see that many of the people receiving them wouldn't have been able to write and get paid for it before. Furthermore, online publishing allows written news to keep up better with current events in a way that only TV and radio could before. If there is a major world crisis, there will be developing articles posted right away at multiple news outlets and updated in real time.

Of course, the lower cost of online publishing means that more people can do it. Greater quantity does not guarantee greater quality. That's one of the tradeoffs of new technology in this case. But it's not as if there weren't outrageously biased news outlets and commentators before the internet. On the good side, now someone is more likely to find a quality publication that cares about their culture and interests, and writers have more options as well. It shouldn't be overlooked either that, generally speaking, most people still have a sense that there is a difference of quality between some random person's blog and a *Wall Street Journal* editorial. The industry has changed, and some people have been hurt by that change, but on net the shift is positive not only for people in the business but also for people who previously weren't in the business at all, which include web and IT personnel, social media marketers, consumers, and so on.

To circle back to factories, more machinery does mean less human work ... at those factories ... maybe. What people don't see is that that machinery comes from somewhere. It represents entirely new industries that have been created and that employ many people of their own. And that machinery needs to be maintained by people with the skill and expertise to do so. At the same time, because automation reduces the labor cost of production, it enables companies to lower prices to consumers while still increasing profits. What is a loss for the few is a win for the many.

Technological advancements certainly fall under the same moral limits as other human endeavors (including, perhaps most importantly, the personalist insistence never to treat a person as a means to an end). However, at their best, they represent one of the finest examples of the image of God shining through humanity. Not only do people make things from God's world, they make things *that make things* from his world. Such achievements require long processes of trial and error by people especially gifted with the intelligence, intuition, and patience necessary to see a project through, even after many failures, for the benefit of humankind.

One of the cradles of invention in the medieval era was monasteries, communities of people who dedicated their lives to being "renewed in knowledge according to the image of Him who created [them]" (Col. 3:10). Monks created and adopted new technology, much of which we still benefit from today, such as clocks, mills, and double-entry bookkeeping. They did this out of self-interest, wanting simply to keep track of the hours of prayer, more productively use their resources and pay their bills, and balance their accounts. But the benefits could not be contained to them alone. So, too, with any other technology. Despite the protests of neo-Luddites, technology really does improve our lives and our economies, and thereby serves the common good.[13]

Inequality

Most people who worry about inequality don't want an absurd world like "Harrison Bergeron," but often people don't see that the inequality they do want to eliminate would require similarly drastic measures. Most often what people decry is economic inequality, sometimes under the even more problematic rubric of income inequality. (Remember the discussion of income versus consumption measures in chapter 3?) The point of this section is not that all inequality, or even all economic inequality, is good, but only that *inequality may be either just or unjust.* Thus, we err if we assume that the mere fact of inequality signifies social injustice.

Yet, if there is one thing that religious leaders around the world seem to agree on today, it is the evils of income inequality stemming from a globalized economy. Pope Francis said in his apostolic exhortation *Evangelii Gaudium* that "we ... have to say 'thou shalt not' to an economy of exclusion and inequality. Such an economy kills."[14] Ecumenical Patriarch Bartholomew of the Orthodox Church wrote in his 2012 Christmas encyclical that "the gloomy consequences of the overconcentration of wealth in the hands of the few and the financial desolation of the vast human masses are ignored. This disproportion, which is described worldwide as a financial crisis, is essentially the product of a moral crisis."[15]

Setting aside the fact that this is not what is meant by the term *financial crisis*, it would seem the spiritual consensus is that economic inequalities have increased worldwide, and this is a clear moral evil. But when we examine the numbers, a somewhat different picture emerges. Even as inequality has increased, extreme poverty has simultaneously decreased—a clear moral good. Moreover, that good likely would not be possible without inequality.

That inequalities are growing is indeed borne out by the facts. *The World Bank History of Global Income Inequality Working*

Report states that from 1988 to 2008, "among the very top of the global income distribution and among the 'emerging global middle class,' which includes more than a third of world population ... we find most significant increases in per capita income." According to this report, the top one percent in the world has enjoyed an increase in real income of more than 60 percent in those two decades.

That is not, however, the end of the story. In fact the biggest increases

> were registered around the median: 80% real increase at the median itself and some 70% around it. It is there, between the 50th and 60th percentile of the global income distribution that we find some 200 million Chinese, 90 million Indians, and about 30 million people each from Indonesia, Brazil and Egypt.

Why only discuss one third of the world's population? What about everybody else? The World Bank report says: "The surprise is that those at the bottom third of the global income distribution have also made significant gains." The real incomes of the people at the bottom third rose between more than 40 percent and almost 70 percent. "The only exception," says the report, is the poorest five percent, "whose real incomes have remained the same."

Now, this still amounts to an increase in global inequality, but it is also really great news for some of the poorest people in the world. The report continues:

> It is this income increase at the bottom of the global pyramid that has allowed the proportion of what the World Bank calls the absolute poor (people whose per capita income is less than 1.25 PPP [purchasing power parity] dollars per day) to go down from 44% to 23% over approximately the same 20 years.

Who, if any, are the real losers—or at least the "nonwinners"— of globalization? It is the "global upper-middle class"; those "between the 75th and 90th percentiles of the global income distribution whose real income gains were essentially nil." The global upper-middle class includes "many from former Communist countries and Latin America, as well as those citizens of rich countries whose incomes stagnated."[16] That the global upper-middle class should be in this situation is certainly cause for concern, but it hardly qualifies as "a moral crisis" of the sort described by the Pope or the Patriarch.

The Credit Suisse Global Wealth Report 2013 confirms that both this high global inequality and the simultaneous increase in global wealth continued even after the 2008 global economic crisis. "Global wealth has reached a new all-time high of USD [United States Dollars] 241 trillion," says the report, which is

> up 4.9% since last year, with the US accounting for most of the rise. Average wealth hit a new peak of USD 51,600 per adult, but inequality remains high, with the top 10% of the world population owning 86% of global wealth, compared to barely 1% for the bottom half of all adults.

While acknowledging continued poverty in developing countries, Credit Suisse also notes:

> Commentaries on wealth often focus exclusively on the top part of the pyramid, which is unfortunate because USD 40 trillion of household wealth is held in the base and middle segments, and satisfying the needs of these asset owners may well drive new trends in consumption, industry and finance. Brazil, China, Korea and Taiwan are countries that are already rising quickly through this part of the wealth pyramid, with Indonesia close behind and India growing fast from a low starting point.[17]

To the World Bank and Credit Suisse reports we can add the 2014 public opinion findings of Barna, the religiously oriented marketing research firm. Despite the fact that "the percentage of people in the world who live in extreme poverty has decreased by more than half," according to Barna, "more than eight in 10 Americans ... are unaware global poverty has reduced so drastically. More than two-thirds ... say they thought global poverty was on the rise over the past three decades."[18] This is what happens when people over-focus on inequality. They are so busy looking at the wealthy that they don't see all the good that is happening with the poor.[19]

What's the payoff from all of this? First, even while global economic inequality has been increasing, global poverty has significantly declined. Thus, the assumption that inequality somehow *requires* suffering, exploitation, and poverty must be rejected. It is simply false. That, thank God, is not the world we live in.

Second, the correlation between the two (rising inequality and decreasing poverty) raises questions of whether there is a connection. Of course, there is. In healthy economies, wealth is constantly being created and the potential for any one person or group of people to get lucky and marvelously profit from it increases at the same time. What this means is that the greater standard of living in an economy, the more unequal we should expect it to be. If a ton of people make $50,000 per year, a few make $1 million, and even fewer make $1 billion, that makes for more inequality than if most people made only $1,000 per year while just a few made $1 million. But in the latter case, most people would be poor, while in the former most would be middle class. Shouldn't that difference matter more than the proportion of total wealth distribution?

Asserting, despite this, that all those who are wealthy are nevertheless evil must assume that moral worth can be measured in money, a warped form of thinking that we know is simply a form of consumerism. On the contrary, recall again the words of St. John Chrysostom: "Neither is wealth an evil, but the having made a bad use of wealth; nor is poverty a virtue, but the having made a virtuous use of poverty."[20] Do some people make "a bad use of wealth"? Yes, some do. Wealth brings with it hosts of temptations. But the charitable (and reasonable) thing to do is to wait to see evidence of bad use in any particular case before assuming it to be there.

Having established this fact, it becomes clearer how we end up back at Harrison Bergeron. In a relatively free economy, everyone has a chance to work his or her way up in life. It doesn't guarantee that everyone will, of course, but it is better than aristocratic or caste societies, where one is confined by law and custom to the class in which one is born. The massive amount of wealth produced in the modern era comes from technological advancement and the expansion of economic liberty in the last two hundred years. To equalize everyone, we'd have to do away with all those things essential to economic liberty: private property, profits, trade, and so on. And none of that would do away with the differences between people that significantly contribute to economic inequality in the first place. The person interested in engineering is likely to have a higher income than a gifted artist. We could try to fix the price of labor so that everyone is paid the same, but we already know that wouldn't work. The only other option is instituting a Handicapper General to do away with every form of diversity in our societies. No thanks.

After all that, however, we must be careful that we do not err in the opposite direction. Not all economic inequality is just. I've already mentioned North Korea in the last chapter, where most people are poor but the government elites live well. But this problem is far more pervasive than that obvious example. I purposefully qualified my statement in the last paragraph with the phrase "in a *relatively* free economy." I need to do this because nearly every economy in the world is a mixed economy to some degree (i.e., neither purely capitalist nor purely socialist). That degree matters a lot. I'd rather live in Seoul, South Korea, than in Beijing, China. And I'd rather live in Beijing than Pyongyang, North Korea, any day. But it is not as if economies like Seoul could not be *more* economically free or that the economic well-being of the poor there doesn't matter, despite their riches compared to the poor in Pyongyang. Relative wealth is no justification to close our eyes to relative poverty and unjust inequality.

What do I mean? Even in some of the freest economies there is inequality generated not through the creation of wealth but through restricting markets to favor parties with political connections—what we referred to as cronyism in chapter 3. I'll examine this problem further in the next two sections.

Rule of Law

Let's look again at Harrison Bergeron. Vonnegut stipulates that in the story's future dystopian society, people "weren't only equal before God and the law. They were equal every which way." Rule of law is about being equal before God and the law. It is the good kind of equality that we want in society. It is the equality of the United States *Declaration of Independence*: "We hold these truths to be self-evident, that all men are created equal, that they are endowed by their Creator with certain unalienable Rights, that among these are Life, Liberty and the pursuit of Happiness."[21]

The idea of rule of law predates the United States, of course. But it is the first modern country to put it so front and center. As we saw in chapter 2, without the rule of law there is tyranny. Equality before the law means even royalty and aristocrats and generals and law enforcement are subject to the same body of law as ordinary citizens. It also means that majorities are subject to the same laws as minorities. It is the origin of the idea of government officials as public servants rather than rulers. The law is the ruler, and everyone is subject to it.

In practice, of course, the rule of law requires constant struggle to maintain. People try to undermine it all the time. Usually those people don't want—or at least pretend they don't want—to be tyrants. Instead, they want to protect domestic jobs from foreign competition, so they subsidize domestic products. This is another harm of being allergic to trade. Subsidizing an industry creates unseen opportunity costs. In particular, it undermines the rule of law by treating one domestic industry differently than others. This may mean treating certain established companies in one industry differently than their upstart competitors, but even if the subsidy is available to every business in an industry, that still means more people and resources will be attracted to that industry than they would have been otherwise. This, in fact, is the point of the subsidy. Another way to put it is that *inefficiency and unjust, artificial inequality are the point of subsidies.*

By treating industries unequally through subsidies, one industry is propped up at the expense of all the others. If corn or oil weren't subsidized in the United States, for example, those industries would suffer losses. But because everyone would see that they were no longer as profitable as they thought, more people would invest resources by pursuing other crops or energy sources or, for that matter, anything else. The opportunity cost reaches far beyond the ability of substitute goods to compete with one industry. Those additional resources might be invested in developing an innovative and inexpensive new way to improve sanitation in developing countries. Or they could invest in companies making new and entertaining smart phone apps. Or people could be creating new ways to travel or communicate or farm or cultivate quality time with family or some other innovation that most people can't even imagine but would change their quality of life for the better if only the right entrepreneurs had the resources they needed. So long as all businesses don't enjoy equality before the law when it comes to subsidies, there will always be losses like these.

At least with subsidies unequal treatment comes through *manipulating* the law—there is still some reverence for the law itself, even if it is unequally written. And it's out there for everyone to see, if they know to look for it. More insidious violations of the rule of law come in the form of bribery and corruption. Osvaldo Schenone and the Acton Institute's director of research Samuel Gregg explored this problem in their monograph *A Theory of Corruption*, writing,

> Though corruption is associated with the original sin that marks the heart of every person, corruption is also a social scourge that debilitates the daily economic and legal transactions upon which all of us ultimately depend for our material survival. For many people corruption is invisible, as it is often limited to specific sectors of the economy. For others, it is an omnipresent feature of their existence. In all cases, however, corruption is ultimately derived from the personal choices of individuals to violate the law that, as Saint Paul reminds us, is written on our hearts.[22]

What is corruption? Schenone and Gregg point out that it is not simply a synonym for crime. "Tax evasion, for example, is a crime, but it is not corruption. However, bribing a tax-auditor is corruption because there is a voluntary transaction between the evader and the auditor with the intention of defrauding a third party (the government)."[23] Thus, corruption violates legal justice. While insisting (rightly) that the most important solution is the transformation of people's hearts, because corruption is ultimately a sin, the authors also insist, "This, however, is no excuse for ignoring the distorted moral and institutional ecology produced by sin."[24]

Accordingly, they detail the most common institutional effects of corruption:

> Economists are virtually unanimous in illustrating that while corruption can grow everywhere, the most fertile soil is found in the public sector. Private corporations, for example, cannot create tariff barriers or customs collections.... In other words, the state facilitates some of the conditions for corruption by legislating that certain things must be done in certain ways, or that various duties ought to be paid, or that particular permits must be obtained. Some people will try to circumvent these barriers by paying a bribe, but, if such duties and permits did not exist in the first place, the incentives for corruption would be significantly diminished.[25]

This does not mean that corruption can be eradicated through external means—it is, at base, a matter of the heart. But it does mean the more a state imposes such regulations, the greater opportunity and incentive there will be for corruption. At its worst, this means that trying to legally do some of the simplest things, like start a business, can take days, weeks, or even months. The arduous process becomes a means for extortion. Though bribery is itself a sin, the person *receiving the bribe* is the person with the power in the relationship. He or she is equally, if not more, guilty. When an industry is overregulated, some people find themselves with seemingly no choice but to bribe and may do so only under duress.

Perhaps ironically, then, we can say that societies and sectors of societies that lack the rule of law tend to have more laws. These laws are used to impose what the economist Kenneth Boulding called a threat system where what happens is not a voluntary exchange or a favor but an ultimatum: that is, "give me this bribe or I'll shut down your business."[26] It is a system of social organization inherently built on relationships of fear and intimidation. The rule of law is undermined not when there are few laws but when laws are used to undermine equality "before God and the law." While "Harrison Bergeron" is science fiction, the absence of the rule of law is a terrifying reality many live with today. Same planet, same dimension. And there is no society entirely free from corruption, just as there is no person entirely free from sin. This last point may sound pessimistic, but it actually should take some weight off our shoulders. Eradicating every opportunity for corruption is impossible, but that means that we need not be perfectionistic. We only need to keep corruption to a low enough level that the rule of law remains the general norm for freedom to be possible in society.

Free Markets

There is a phrase popular among clergy of all traditions that I find utterly puzzling. Always used negatively, that phrase is "unfettered markets." Unfettered markets are blamed for the 2008 financial crisis, for unjust inequality (often assumed to be all inequality), for poverty, for environmental degradation, and so on. They can seem, in the statements of these theologians, to be as insidious as the devil and as ubiquitous as sin. However, I've yet to see the term defined with any clarity or precision, and from the sound of it my inclination is to think that unfettered markets is something we need more of, not less.

To recall the insights of Walter Eucken from chapter 3, remember that free markets are open markets. They are markets with as few barriers to entry as possible. As such, any given economy may have all kinds of markets with varying degrees of freedom. In the United States, most people will immediately recognize that the market for startups in Silicon Valley is much freer than the markets for cable companies or healthcare or construction. What we need are *fewer* fetters on our markets, so that anyone who wants to compete will not face too many artificial barriers keeping them out, thus diminishing the good stewardship of the world's resources and preventing the creation of new wealth and jobs that did not previously exist.

Chaining down markets means chaining down small businesses and would-be entrepreneurs because the only market actors that can wade through overregulated markets are big, established ones. Only they can afford the legal teams needed to comply with every such restriction on commerce. That is why in some cases these firms will even lobby for higher taxes or licensing requirements or zoning laws or subsidies or unneeded safety codes or ineffective but arduous environmental standards. They know that every such regulation is another barrier to entry for a potential competitor, making their supply monopoly or oligopoly in the market more secure.

"Liberty," wrote Lord Acton, "is not a means to a higher political end. It is itself the highest political end. It is not for the sake of a good public administration that it is required, but for security in the pursuit of the highest objects of civil society, and of private life."[27] Acton is quick to point out that the beneficial consequences of liberty are not always certain. In some cases, he even admits that a despot might more effectively solve any given social problem in the short term. But what goes unseen is the long-term cost of forfeiting freedom. Liberty is the highest political end because it creates the space for every individual and institution of society to pursue the highest objects of civil society, and of private life.

Open markets do not guarantee competition. Being able to take the risk of entrepreneurship in any given market does not guarantee success. In fact, we can even say that it makes failure more likely, because open markets mean markets without protections from failure for businesses. The vitality of free markets, and thus of free economies, depends on people who have the courage (a cardinal virtue!) to take risks for the sake of developing their God-given creativity in ways that serve human needs.

Another way to put this highlights the "What if?" side of this issue: Free markets exclude discrimination; unfree, fettered markets enable it. In this way, regulations such as protected class status for religion, race, gender, and nation of origin are procompetitive regulations because they keep these things from being barriers to entry. Do we want industries to be able to discriminate against upstarts on the basis of these things? Ironically, if freedom and fairness are truly our goals, the only good regulations on markets are ones that *remove* fetters rather than create them.

While most people would (or, at least, should) agree that discrimination on the basis of religion or race or gender is undesirable, what goes unseen are fewer politically charged but far more common bases of discrimination. The most common one is simply when established firms don't want to compete anymore and so discriminate against all potential competitors. Not all established firms do this, of course. I'd hate to encourage that prejudice. But when it does happen, instead of competing in free markets such companies lobby for artificial barriers to entry that go beyond the barriers everyone would normally face, such as developing a competitive product, organizing a business plan, and raising enough startup capital.

Beyond these natural barriers are artificial, external barriers, such as the following. Increased corporate and property taxes create additional startup and maintenance costs, which new enterprises are at a disadvantage to pay. Licensing requirements not only add financial costs but also considerable costs of time. The state of Louisiana, for example, requires 750 hours of classes to become a licensed cosmetologist, and it requires the license even for professions such as the Asian art of eyebrow threading that aren't actually taught in any of the classes and pose no safety concerns.[28] (For that matter, what concerns merit requiring a cosmetology license for actual cosmetologists in the first place?) Zoning laws tell people what they can and can't use their land for and how. Safety and environmental regulations may sometimes be justified, but they often aren't, and in all cases they add extra compliance costs.

Markets with especially onerous versions of these regulations, or simply with a bad enough combination of smaller ones, become hostile to new enterprise. Such regulations are like the tares in Jesus's parable that an enemy sows in his competitor's field (see Matthew 13:24–30, 36–43). Those were weeds in the fertile soil of faith. These are weeds in the fertile soil of freedom.

Almost every "What if?" before this one has been foundational for it as well. Without private property, profits, free prices, money, trade, (just) inequality, and the rule of law, we cannot have free markets either. And technology not only enables wealth creation but is the fruit of it. In some of these cases, we can't even have markets without them at all. But without free markets, even if only in various, imperfect degrees, we wouldn't have the widespread growth in human flourishing we've experienced over the last two hundred years nor any hope of it continuing for the next two hundred.

Moreover, without free markets, rightly understood, we wouldn't have freedom in society at all. What is freedom of speech if not a free market of speech? What is freedom of the press if not a free market of publication? What is freedom of religion if not a free market of religion? What is democracy if not a free market of politics?

Acton's caution is an important one. Freedom doesn't guarantee the most desirable results in the short term. But without it, we strangle our own potential and the potential of everyone else in our societies—not only the rich and the powerful but also the poor, the vulnerable, and the marginalized. We can try to force the results we want, but in so doing we unjustly elevate one group of society at the expense of others. Free markets and economies, by contrast, are not zero-sum games. They are economic and social win-wins. They are thus the cornerstone of everything admirable in the classical liberal tradition, which itself was the delicate fruit, achieved only after great striving and many failures, of Christian civilization. We would not be better off without them.

Discussion Questions

1. What if we didn't have trade? How does trade affect your life? How do you benefit from it?

2. What's your favorite technology? What did it take to create it? What would the world be missing without it?

3. When is inequality a good thing? When is it unjust?

4. Why is the rule of law important? Have you ever experienced the effects of corruption in your own life? If so, how?

5. In what ways do people try to fetter free markets? What is the effect? What is lost when markets are encumbered by artificial barriers to entry? What is lost when we don't have free markets?

Notes

1. John Emerich Edward Dalberg-Acton, "The History of Freedom in Antiquity," in *Essays in the History of Liberty: Selected Writings of Lord Acton*, vol. 1, ed. J. Rufus Fears (Indianapolis: Liberty Fund, 1985), 5.

2. Kurt Vonnegut, Jr., "Harrison Bergeron," in Vonnegut, Jr., *Welcome to the Monkey House* (New York: Random House/Dial Press, 2010), 7.

3. Dana Frank, *Buy American: The Untold Story of Economic Nationalism* (Boston: Beacon Press, 1999), 160.

4. Frank, *Buy American*, 161.

5. Adam Smith, *An Inquiry into the Nature and Causes of the Wealth of Nations*, vol. 1, Glasgow Edition of the Works of Adam Smith, vol. 2 (Oxford: Oxford University Press, 1976; repr., Indianapolis, IN: LibertyClassics, 1981), 456–57. Henceforth: *Wealth of Nations*.

6. Smith, *Wealth of Nations*, 1:458.

7. Smith, *Wealth of Nations*, 1:458.

8. "How Much of Your Car Is Made in America," *Consumer Reports*, June 15, 2011, http://www.consumerreports.org/cro/news/2011/06/how-much-of-your-car-is-made-in-america/index.htm.

9. For a critique of Berry's activism against modern agricultural technology by a fan of his literary work, see Bruce Edward Walker, "Wendell Berry: Great Poet, Cranky Luddite on Ag Tech," *Acton Commentary*, May 25, 2016, http://www.acton.org/pub/commentary/2016/05/25/wendell-berry-great-poet-cranky-luddite-ag-tech.

10. See Ben Casselman, "Manufacturing Jobs Are Never Coming Back," *FiveThirtyEight*, March 18, 2016, http://fivethirtyeight.com/features/manufacturing-jobs-are-never-coming-back/.

11. Ken Doctor, "Newsonomics: The Halving of America's Daily Newsrooms," *Newsonomics*, July 28, 2015, http://newsonomics.com/newsonomics-the-halving-of-americas-daily-newsrooms/.

12. Michael Barthel, "5 Key Takeaways about the State of the News Media in 2016," *Pew Research Center*, June 15, 2016, http://www.pewresearch.org/fact-tank/2016/06/15/state-of-the-news-media-2016-key-takeaways/.

13. This section on technology is a revision of an essay I wrote on the subject. See Dylan Pahman, "Technology, Seen and Unseen," *Acton Commentary*, August 10, 2016, https://acton.org/pub/commentary/2016/08/10/technology-seen-and-unseen.

14. Pope Francis, Apostolic Exhortation *Evangelii Gaudium*, 53, November 24, 2013, http://w2.vatican.va/content/francesco/en/apost_exhortations/documents/papa-francesco_esortazione-ap_20131124_evangelii-gaudium.html#No_to_an_economy_of_exclusion.

15. Ecumenical Patriarch Bartholomew I, "Patriarchal Proclamation of Christmas 2012," December 24, 2012, https://www.patriarchate.org/-/patriarchike-apodeixis-epi-tois-christougennois-2012-. To the extent the Pope and the Patriarch are concerned with exclusion, I agree with them. However, it is an error to simply presume that inequality necessarily comes about through exclusion.

16. Branko Milanovic, *Global Income Inequality by the Numbers: In History and Now—An Overview*, World Bank Group, November 2012, http://elibrary.worldbank.org/doi/abs/10.1596/1813-9450-6259.

17. *Global Wealth Report 2013*, Credit Suisse, October 2013, https://publications.credit-suisse.com/tasks/render/file/?fileID=BCDB1364-A105-0560-1332EC9100FF5C83.

18. *Global Poverty Is on the Decline, but Almost No One Believes It*, Barna Group, April 28, 2014, https://www.barna.org/barna-update/culture/668-global-poverty-is-on-the-decline-but-almost-no-one-believes-it#.V5-szKI1vEl.

19. The previous paragraphs on economic inequality are adapted from an essay I wrote on the subject. See Dylan Pahman, "Impoverished Pontifications, Part I," *Library of Law and Liberty*, August 7, 2014, http://www.libertylawsite.org/2014/08/07/impoverished-pontifications-part-one/.

20. John Chrysostom, *Homily against Publishing the Errors of the Brethren*, in *NPNF*[1] 9:236.

21. United States Congress, *The Declaration of Independence*, July 4, 1776, available at http://www.archives.gov/exhibits/charters/declaration_transcript.html.

22. Osvaldo Schenone and Samuel Gregg, *A Theory of Corruption* (Grand Rapids: Acton Institute, 2003), 1.

23. Schenone and Gregg, *A Theory of Corruption*, 1–2.

24. Schenone and Gregg, *A Theory of Corruption*, 11.

25. Schenone and Gregg, *A Theory of Corruption*, 13.

26. For an introduction to the concept of threat systems, see Kenneth Boulding, "Towards a Pure Theory of Threat Systems," *The American Economic Review* 53, no. 2 (May 1963): 424–34. Not all threat systems are bad. Law in general, in fact, is a threat system.

27. Acton, "The History of Freedom in Antiquity," 22.

28. See Eric Boehm, "Louisiana's Licensing Laws Nearly Destroyed This Woman's Eyebrow Threading Business: Now She's Fighting Back," *Reason*, August 2, 2016, http://reason.com/blog/2016/08/02/louisianas-licensing-laws-eyebrow-busine.

Conclusion

My picture of man is fashioned by the spiritual heritage of classical and Christian tradition. I see in man the likeness of God; I am profoundly convinced that it is an appalling sin to reduce man to a means (even in the name of high-sounding phrases) and that each man's soul is something unique, irreplaceable, priceless, in comparison with which all other things are as naught.

—Wilhelm Röpke[1]

Closing the Curtain

Coming now to the end of this little book, I must do my duty and review what has already been said. I consider this a great service to potential readers who may not know whether they want to spend their time and money on such a book and would like to skip to the end and read the short version before determining if they want to read the whole thing.

Writing, after all, is a vocation. That means that it is not only a gift from God (and it is), but also that it shouldn't serve itself alone. Over this, too, I am called to be a child of God and a steward of what he has given me, just like any other property I own.

My goal has been to give readers the tools they need to begin to engage in the enterprise of Christian social thought, to gain a biblical and theological take on our relationships, as beings created in the divine image, to God, to ourselves, to others, and to the rest of creation without steamrolling over the prudential insights of economic science. Another way of putting this, however, is to say that I have written a small treatise on theological anthropology in part 1 (with specific concern for how it can be used to develop a paradigm for social analysis and action) and examined a few basic economic insights in part 2.

In the introduction, I outlined the fundamental problem of disconnecting good intentions from sound economics. I used the example of fair trade coffee to show that simply wanting to do the right thing is not enough when it comes to economic questions. Conversely, drawing on economist Frank Knight, among others, I insisted that while life is economic, economics is not all of life. A proper Christian anthropology needs to include both the spiritual and the material aspects of our lives.

To that end, in the first chapter, I looked at what it means for each individual human person to be created in the image of God. In short, like God, we are free, creative, rational, and capable of virtue. Like the rest of creation, we are bounded by time and space; conditioned by change, growth, and loss; and in our rationality we must attend to the fact that we are also bodily, material, and passionate. Human persons are soul-body unities, and the severing of this relationship results in the tragic and unnatural state of death. We were meant to change and grow, but through sin we are corrupted and die. Since we can't save ourselves from death, we need a Savior to do that for us: Jesus Christ who conquers sin and death through his cross and resurrection. In Christ we are able to become, once again, what God meant for us to become. As my friend Christina once said, Jesus shows us that the correct answer to the question, "What does it mean to be human?" is another question: "Who is Jesus Christ?" Because we are not omniscient, that is a question deeper than our own souls, to which I expect we will be discovering more and more true and amazing answers all throughout eternity.

In the second chapter, I looked at what the image of God means for our relationship to other human persons. The short answer is that other people can be annoying, but it turns out we need and even (sometimes) want each other. We are social beings. That social life is not immune to the corrupting effects of sin and death, and it needs redemption as much as our own souls. By putting the inviolable dignity of the human person first, we can see that while we naturally group together and while community is a good thing, we cannot sacrifice the individual to the group, nor the group to the individual. Rather, freedom in society protects the individual and strengthens our communities, spheres, and societies. God has given us a law written on our hearts, and the best of human laws seek to apply that law to our particular social contexts, conditioned by time, place, and our own maturity. Furthermore, God has given us grace through his Son and in his body, the church. Thus, for the redemption of our social lives, religious liberty ought to be of primary importance. Without freedom of conscience, we cannot have any other freedom.

In the third chapter, I looked at what the image of God means for our relationship to the rest of creation. Just as good parents do not want their children to trash the house, so also God does not want us to trash the world. Instead, he calls us to stewardship in our property and virtue in our consumption (or use) of it. Human economies are meant to be the cultivation of creation, through human labor, for the provision of human needs, through relationships of exchange. Networks of exchange are called markets, and an economy is a massive web of markets. Markets can be diverse or monopolistic, but the most important thing is that they be open or free. In free markets, new participants face the fewest barriers to entry and the greatest opportunity for the creation of wealth, which since the Industrial Revolution has improved the living conditions of billions of our neighbors throughout the world. Economics is not all of life, and the life of the spirit must never be sacrificed for material gain. But free markets best accord with our natures as free and social beings, and they have the greatest potential for improving the plight of the poor among us. It would certainly be a failure of judgment to claim that such a thing had no spiritual value. Indeed, it not only serves the common good but the kingdom of God, to the extent that it enables us to better spread the love of the gospel throughout the world.

In chapter 4, we moved to the application section of the book, examining what life would look like without private property, profits, free prices, and money. In chapter 5, we did the same thing with trade, technology, inequality, rule of law, and free markets. The answers varied in their horribleness, but in general we concluded that a world without these things would be some variety of dystopian hellscape. *Brave New World, 1984, The Hunger Games*—stories such as these are entertaining when they are fictional, but when they take place on the same planet and in the same dimension that we live in, they are tragic. Furthermore, all of these important institutions and properties of free economies and societies come in degrees. In any given society, there is always room for improvement—and for corruption. This makes the task of upholding and strengthening them all the more important. We should not take these things for granted. Liberty truly is "the delicate fruit of a mature civilization."[2]

My hope and prayer is that this little book, which has come into your hands through the labor of countless people and communities created in the image of God and through a series of exchanges made possible by economic freedom, would contribute in some small way to this end: promoting a free and virtuous society for the kingdom of God and the common good of all.

—Dylan Pahman

Notes

1. Wilhelm Röpke, *A Humane Economy: The Social Framework of the Free Market*, trans. Elizabeth Henderson (Chicago: Henry RegneryCompany, 1960), 5.

2. John Emerich Edward Dalberg-Acton, "The History of Freedom in Antiquity," in *Essays in the History of Liberty: Selected Writings of Lord Acton*, vol. 1, ed. J. Rufus Fears (Indianapolis: Liberty Fund, 1985), 5.

Appendix

The Acton Institute's Core Principles

Dignity of the Person—The human person, created in the image of God, is individually unique, rational, the subject of moral agency, and a co-creator. Accordingly, he possesses intrinsic value and dignity, implying certain rights and duties both for himself and other persons. These truths about the dignity of the human person are known through revelation, but they are also discernible through reason.

Social Nature of the Person—Although persons find ultimate fulfillment only in communion with God, one essential aspect of the development of persons is our social nature and capacity to act for disinterested ends. The person is fulfilled by interacting with other persons and by participating in moral goods. There are voluntary relations of exchange, such as market transactions that realize economic value. These transactions may give rise to moral value as well. There are also voluntary relations of mutual dependence, such as promises, friendships, marriages, and the family, which are moral goods. These, too, may have other sorts of value, such as religious, economic, aesthetic, and so on.

Importance of Social Institutions—Because persons are by nature social, various human persons develop social institutions. The institutions of civil society, especially the family, are the primary sources of a society's moral culture. These social institutions are neither created by nor derive their legitimacy from the state. The state must respect their autonomy and provide the support necessary to ensure the free and orderly operation of all social institutions in their respective spheres.

Human Action—Human persons are by nature acting persons. Through human action, the person can actualize his potentiality by freely choosing the moral goods that fulfill his nature.

Sin—Although human beings in their created nature are good, in their current state, they are fallen and corrupted by sin. The reality of sin makes the state necessary to restrain evil. The ubiquity of sin, however, requires that the state be limited in its power and jurisdiction. The persistent reality of sin requires that we be skeptical of all utopian "solutions" to social ills such as poverty and injustice.

Rule of Law and the Subsidiary Role of Government—The government's primary responsibility is to promote the common good, that is, to maintain the rule of law, and to preserve basic duties and rights. The government's role is not to usurp free actions, but to minimize those conflicts that may arise when the free actions of persons and social institutions result in competing interests. The state should exercise this responsibility according to the principle of subsidiarity. This principle has two components. First, jurisdictionally broader institutions must refrain from usurping the proper functions that should be performed by the person and institutions more immediate to him. Second, jurisdictionally broader institutions should assist individual persons and institutions more immediate to the person only when the latter cannot fulfill their proper functions.

Creation of Wealth—Material impoverishment undermines the conditions that allow humans to flourish. The best means of reducing poverty is to protect private property rights through the rule of law. This allows people to enter into voluntary exchange circles in which to express their creative nature. Wealth is created when human beings creatively transform matter into resources. Because human beings can create wealth, economic exchange need not be a zero-sum game.

Economic Liberty—Liberty, in a positive sense, is achieved by fulfilling one's nature as a person by freely choosing to do what one ought. Economic liberty is a species of liberty so-stated. As such, the bearer of economic liberty not only has certain rights, but also duties. An economically free person, for example, must be free to enter the market voluntarily. Hence, those who have the power to interfere with the market are duty-bound to remove any artificial barrier to entry in the market, and also to protect private and shared property rights. But the economically free person will also bear the duty to others to participate in the market as a moral agent and in accordance with moral goods. Therefore, the law must guarantee private property rights and voluntary exchange.

Economic Value—In economic theory, economic value is subjective because its existence depends on it being felt by a subject. Economic value is the significance that a subject attaches to a thing whenever he perceives a causal connection between this thing and the satisfaction of a present, urgent want. The subject may be wrong in his value judgment by attributing value to a thing that will not or cannot satisfy his present, urgent want. The truth of economic value judgments is settled just in case that thing can satisfy the expected want. While this does not imply the realization of any other sort of value, something can have both subjective economic value and objective moral value.

Priority of Culture—Liberty flourishes in a society supported by a moral culture that embraces the truth about the transcendent origin and destiny of the human person. This moral culture leads to harmony and to the proper ordering of society. While the various institutions within the political, economic, and other spheres are important, the family is the primary inculcator of the moral culture in a society.

Acknowledgments

My biggest thanks are due to my wife Kelly, who is my biggest fan, who persistently supports me, and who dreams big impractical dreams that a boring man like myself would never dare to imagine. I'm equally indebted to my two sons, Brendan and Aidan, who don't know or much care what it is I do or have accomplished and who faithfully remind me on a daily basis that I'm not as great as I like to think I am.

Next to them, I owe immeasurable gratitude to my friends and colleagues: Jordan Ballor, who took a chance on a friend of a friend and got me in at Acton; Dan Hugger, who gave invaluable feedback by reading over early drafts of this book's chapters; and Samuel Gregg, who supported this project from the start. I'd also like to thank Andrew McGinnis, for giving me his office; Marc Scaturro, for this book's amazing cover; Nathan Jacobs, for encouraging my academic pursuits since I was an undergrad; and Kevin Schmiesing, my colleague and editor, who helped this book be better than I ever could have made it on my own.

I'm thankful for my parents, without whom I would not exist, for their love and support, and for all the rest of my family too.

I'm thankful for my many friends who will be very surprised to learn that I wrote a book at all.

I'm thankful for everyone who reads this book.

And I'm thankful to God, for giving me the quirky curiosity to always ask, "Why?" and "So what?" ... even to the point of being annoying.

Gloria in excelsis Deo.

About the Author

Dylan Pahman is a research fellow at the Acton Institute for the Study of Religion & Liberty, where he serves as managing editor of the *Journal of Markets & Morality*. He earned his MTS in Historical Theology from Calvin Theological Seminary in Grand Rapids, Michigan. From 2013-2017, he was also a fellow of the Sophia Institute: International Center for Orthodox Thought and Culture. Dylan is husband to Kelly and father of Brendan and Aidan. You can follow him on Twitter at @DylanPahman and enjoy his tweets about theology, spirituality, philosophy, politics, economics, comics, video games, and late '90s/early 2000s rock music. You can find more of his writing at www.dylanpahman.com.

47807312R00095

Made in the USA
Middletown, DE
03 September 2017